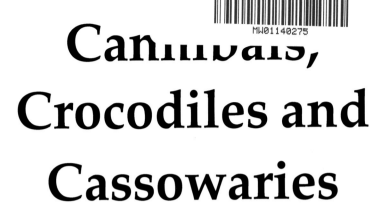

Cannibals, Crocodiles and Cassowaries

A New Zealand Forest Ranger in the
Jungles of Papua New Guinea

Ross Lockyer

Text and images copyright Ross Lockyer 2018
Cover by Sri Lockyer

ISBN 978-0-473-43618-6

Website: www.rosslockyer.co.nz

Published by Ross Lockyer

Contents

Introduction

People have been telling me for about thirty years that I should write a book about my life and adventures around the world. Having procrastinated for years, I was finally motivated to start writing upon re-reading a twelve-page article printed in *New Zealand Logger* magazine in May 2006, entitled "Ross Lockyer—Logging Adventurer".

I had never thought of myself as an "adventurer" until the article in the magazine labelled me as such, but looking back on a full, exciting, and satisfying life and career spent in many different countries and a wide range of environments, I guess that I did have some interesting adventures, and I certainly do have some stories to tell.

I was born and grew up in Taranaki, New Zealand, in the small rural village of Okato, which is some 26 kilometres south of New Plymouth on what is known as "The Coast Road". Okato is about five kilometres from the coast on one side, five kilometres from the Egmont National Park on the other, and is located in the heart of Taranaki dairy country. I spent much of my youth milking cows after school, and trapping possums, and shooting goats on the slopes of Mt Egmont and the adjacent Pouakai Ranges. I left school at 17, joined the New Zealand Forest Service, and spent the next four years training to become a Forest Ranger.

My first book, entitled *The Making of a Forest Ranger*, covers my New Zealand years, including my Taranaki childhood, and my years at Forest Ranger School and with the New Zealand Forest Service.

This second book explores my life and adventures from 1967 to 1973 in Papua New Guinea (PNG). Further books are currently in the pipeline.

This is a story about my own experiences while living and working in PNG, and although I have tried to provide some background prior to the time and situation as I found it in the late 1960s, there is no way I can do justice to the complexities of the local history and cultures in a book such as this. Many others have made some pretty good attempts though, and it's worth seeking them out if you are interested. Both examples mentioned below are worth a look.

In 1968, the Australian National Film Unit arrived in Bulolo with the plan to film a documentary. The subject was Bulolo starting from its gold dredging days through to the then-present day klinkii pine logging operations and ply mill, and the effect of these industries on the Watuts and Kukukukus who live in the Bulolo Valley. The film was to be called *Forest Without Spears*.

I was involved in setting up the CNGT logging and plantation thinning operations for filming, and Ike Samuels and I arranged for the headman of Patankahaua village, Ninka, to recruit some Kukukuku head-hunters from the interior. Ninka and his group of Kukukukus arrived in our logging area in full battle regalia ready to enact a battle scene among the klinkii pines. The resulting film was very well done, and copies of *Forest Without Spears* can be obtained from the Australian National Film Unit.

The very next year, a group of Australian photographers arrived and asked for help to find locations, subjects, and scenes for a book that they were writing and photographing on PNG. I spent quite some time showing them around some suitable locations. I eventually received a personally dedicated copy of the final book, which is a beautifully done photographic record of life in Papua New Guinea in 1969. The book is simply called *New Guinea* and is photographed by Robin Smith and written by Keith Willey.

New Guinea, Here I Come!

When I was encouraged by my girlfriend at the time to get involved in judo at the YMCA gym in Tokoroa, New Zealand, I never imagined that I would end up getting my kneecap kicked off during a training bout. At the time, I was working as a Forest Ranger for New Zealand Forest Products in Tokoroa in the Central North Island of New Zealand. With my left leg in an aluminium cast for nearly three months, I was not able to work out in the field so was transferred to the aerial photography interpretation and harvest planning office.

I had begun to realize that there were other forests out there in the big wide world that were more challenging to a young Forest Ranger than the mono-culture of New Zealand radiata pine plantations, but how to go about finding them? During that time in the office, I came across some back copies of *The Commonwealth Forestry Review*. In the back of some of these I found advertisements for forestry positions in some British Commonwealth countries, so I started sending off letters to addresses in countries as diverse as Sierra Leone, Ceylon, and Papua New Guinea. I knew absolutely nothing about any of these places, but what the hell—I had nothing to lose, and anywhere had to be more interesting than living in Tokoroa!

In June 1967, I was sent a one-way ticket from Auckland to Sydney where I attended interviews with the senior management of Commonwealth New Guinea Timbers Ltd (CNGT) at their head office on Circular Quay. I was offered the position of Forest Ranger/Forest Engineer with CNGT, based in Bulolo, Papua New Guinea. We discussed salary and terms, and I accepted a contract for an initial period of 21 months, followed by three months paid leave.

I can still remember arriving in Port Moresby in July 1967, walking off the plane onto the tarmac, and the heat and humidity hitting me like a wet sandbag! I thought I had walked into the exhaust of the jet engines, but no—it was just the normal PNG midday heat and humidity.

I thought, "What the hell have I let myself in for?"

I stayed in Moresby for only a couple of hours (I learned later that this was about the maximum time that anyone should stay in Port Moresby) and then caught a connecting flight north to Bulolo in the Central Highlands.

I was met at the Bulolo airport by a CNGT representative, ushered into this weird looking car (I had never seen a Volvo before!), and was taken to the CNGT offices where I was introduced to Rod Wheedon, the General Manager. He gave me a rundown on the company and the town and explained where I fitted into the scheme of things.

I was then taken to a *donga,* which is a small bungalow of the type that was allocated to single, senior staff. The cookhouse was 200 metres down the hill, and this supplied breakfast, dinner, and a cut lunch. The whole set-up seemed very civilised.

Bulolo has a fascinating history and was an interesting and pleasant place in which to live and work. Situated in the heart of Morobe Province, its location at around 600 metres above sea level makes for temperatures that are very equable both day and night and extremely comfortable for the tropics.

Until 1914, New Guinea was a German colony (German New Guinea), but after the First World War it became an Australian Mandated Territory. The German administration had discouraged prospecting, but despite this, the presence of gold in the Morobe District was well known. In 1913, a prospector named Darling found good deposits of gold in the Bulolo River area, and some years after the war ended the area around Bulolo became awash with miners and prospectors. In 1926, Guinea Gold No Liability (Guinea Gold NL) was formed to take up leases at Koranga and Bulolo.

Originally, the only method of transporting supplies to the Bulolo Valley was by using native carriers over precipitous tracks from the north coast. The expense of the goods on reaching the goldfields reflected the arduous manner of transporting them. It would take the carriers eight days to trek over the rough tracks from Salamaua on the coast to Bulolo carrying loads of up to 23 kilograms, which included their own rice, for the journey.

Routes for road and railway were examined, but all such options were deemed prohibitively expensive. On top of the building costs, the estimated cost of maintaining the routes made these options unfeasible.

The transport problem was solved with the use of aircraft, opening the way for gold dredging in the area. In 1929, a decision was made to fly in all the parts of two modern gold dredges and assemble them on site. The success of this operation during the next few years aroused worldwide interest, as it represented a major advance in the technique of aerial freighting.

The Morobe Goldfield reached its peak production in 1938, when 700 expatriates and 6,218 local miners produced 404,000 ounces of gold. By the mid-1980s, the field had produced 3,500,000 ounces of alluvial gold and 500,000 ounces of hard-rock gold.

The Bulolo Valley was not permanently inhabited before the white man arrived. Apparently the natives avoided it because of the very high incidence of malaria, giving it the name of Death Valley. It was also a no-man's land and hereditary battleground between the Buangs who lived to the north and northeast and the Kukukukus (also known as the Angu or Änga people) who occupied the high country to the south and southwest.

The Kukukukus could probably be classed as pygmies, as they are very short in stature, with an average male height of just over 140 centimetres (pygmy peoples are defined as ethnic populations in which adult men average less than 150 centimetres in height). What they lack in height, however, they make up for in ferocity! The Kukukukus were, and still are, the wildest and most terrifying tribe in the whole of PNG. They are well-known as head hunters and cannibals, and all other tribes are terrified of them and generally avoid them at all costs.

The Bulolo area had extensive stands of excellent timber on the steep hills rising out of the Bulolo Valley and on the watershed between the Bulolo and the upper Watut. The Bulolo Gold Dredging Company (BGD) obtained the timber permits for this area from the early stages of the mining operations. They originally required timber for the construction of housing, workshops, and other buildings from the start-up in 1929, and a sawmill was built at Bulolo to process some of this timber. A larger commercial sawmill was set up in 1946.

The predominant commercial species of note in the area was klinkii pine *(Auracaria hunstenii)*, plus some good but scattered stands of cedar *(Cedrella toona)*, and erima *(Octomeles sumatrana)*. Klinkii pine is a beautiful tree, large in diameter, tall, and as straight as a gun barrel, with at least half of the stem free from knots. Klinkii pine grows to a height of 91.5 metres, and a three metre girth was common. During my time at Bulolo, we dropped one tree that was measured at 85.5 metres, and there were many others that were similar in height. There were stands of hoop pine *(Auracaria cunninghamii)* as well, but these were mainly located at the higher elevations around Wau.

In 1964, when the last gold dredge ground to a halt, Placer Development set up a new company called Commonwealth New Guinea Timbers Ltd to exploit the rich timber resources of the Bulolo and Watut Valleys, and a plymill was constructed at Bulolo.

The logging operations in the Bulolo-Watut forests were designed to feed this plymill and the recently upgraded sawmill, and this is where I was to work for the next four years.

Early on in my career in PNG, I developed an interest in the ethnology, languages, and primitive cultures of the place. I can recall very clearly, as a kid of about ten or twelve, dreaming of being able to converse fluently in another language. I picked up a smattering of Maori from school mates, and I learned French at school, but I was far from fluent in either language. It turned out, however, that I did have a good ear for languages and accents, which—coupled with a good memory and a genuine interest in the culture of the people of the area where I was living—made it relatively easy for me to learn New Guinea Pidgin soon after my arrival in PNG.

Papua New Guinea is one of the most culturally and linguistically diverse countries in the world. There are 852 separate languages listed for the entire country, of which 12 now have no known living speakers. Most of the population of (now) over seven million people live in customary communities as diverse as the languages themselves. It also has one of the most rural populations, as only 18 percent of its people live in urban centres. The country is one of the world's least explored, culturally and geographically, and many undiscovered species of plants and animals are still thought to exist in the interior. In 1967, when I arrived in PNG, there was a total population of about three million people split into some 840 tribes, and each tribe had its own entirely distinctive language unintelligible to any of the other 839. Many of those languages also have numerous dialects, especially if the tribal territory is large and the villages isolated. It was fair to say then, and still is today, that most of the 840 different tribes of PNG lived in a permanent state of suspicion and often aggression with the other 839.

Hence, it was necessary very early in the history of the white man arriving in PNG to establish a lingua franca that would enable not only the white man to communicate with the natives, but the natives of different tribes to communicate with each other. In effect, two different lingua franca emerged. In Papua, the southern half of PNG, the lingua franca is called "Police Motu". That language was established by the Government Patrol Officers or *Kiaps*, as they were known.

In New Guinea, parts of which were more commercially exploited first by the Germans, then the Australians, the lingua franca became "Pidgin", also known as "Pidgin English", "Neo-Melanesian", or *Tok Pisin* in the vernacular. Pidgin is a conglomeration of bastardised English, German, Dutch, and a few native dialect words, with a fair smattering of made-up words thrown in. There are also some words that are common to Indonesian and Malay, although these may have jointly originated from the Dutch. Pidgin is basically a descriptive language, using a truncated vocabulary to describe anything for which there is no specific word.

One great example is *buggerup*, the Pidgin word for broken. And if the item in question is really stuffed beyond repair (which frequently occurs in PNG), and your native worker reports the inevitable, then the phrase is: *"Masta, em i buggerupim tru!"* ("Boss, this thing is completely stuffed!"). That is a phrase that I heard many more times than I would have preferred.

As there was never originally any word for "piano" in PNG (the natives having never seen one before colonisation), a phrase had to be developed when this musical instrument was first introduced into the country, and some good lady's *houseboi* (house and garden servant) got the job of dusting it. Consequently, a piano became: *"Em i wanpela bikpela bilakpela bokis, em i gat sumpela waitpela toots, na i gat sumpela bilakpela toots, na wanpela masta na wanpela missus, em i pait im pait im, na i sing owt nabout"*. It is not too difficult to translate this into English if you read it, but when it is spoken quickly with

15

Pidgin pronunciation it is almost impossible to understand unless you are a Pidgin speaker. The literal translation is: "There is this big black box with some white teeth and some black teeth, and when a white man or white woman strikes it, it produces a nice sound". Quite reasonable really, when you think about it.

Learning Pidgin quickly was an absolute necessity if I was to become effective working and living in PNG. All our native workers, my *houseboi*, and all the natives with whom I came into contact spoke their own tribal language plus Pidgin. When you are immersed in a situation where you must learn the language so that you can do your job or achieve anything at all, and everyone around you speaks it, then it is relatively simple to learn if you put in the effort. I knew of no written dictionary or phrase book available at that time, so I learned to speak Pidgin purely by ear and constant usage.

I discovered in later years that a large part of successfully learning another language is getting the accent right. Because of this, I have been told on many occasions, even when I know that I am far from fluent, "but you are so fluent in our language".

Into the Jungle

Ross Lockyer, Forest Ranger, Commonwealth New Guinea Timbers Ltd, Bulolo, Papua New Guinea. That was me, and at 23 years of age and only 18 months out of Forestry School, I felt a bit like Barry Crump's "Good Keen Man"! Already, PNG was feeling like my kind of country. It was a long way from milking cows on a Taranaki dairy farm, and I was going to make the most of it.

I was issued with my first ever company vehicle a couple of weeks after I started work: a 1942 Willys Jeep. Completely original, it included left-hand drive, crash gearbox, canvas top, no doors, heaps of built-in rattles, and minimal suspension. In fact, it felt like it had no suspension at all on those Bulolo forest roads! It was one of many ex-army Jeeps salvaged from the Americans when they departed PNG after the Second World War.

Although I had my own *donga* to live in, I initially had all my meals at the single-man's cookhouse about 200 metres down the road. A *donga* is, I believe, an Australian Aboriginal name for a bush hut, but it was adopted as the PNG term for a single man's accommodation. My abode was a good sized *donga* with a bedroom, living room, toilet, shower, and a sort of large internal porch at the rear. It was raised up on high piles, had heaps of big windows covered with mosquito netting (no glass), and large overhanging verandahs all round to stop the rain and the sun from coming in. It was designed to keep the interior cool, which it did remarkably well. The practical design of the *donga* coupled with the pleasant climate at 600 metres above sea level meant that I never needed a fan or any other cooling device.

The roomy, under-floor area served as the wash-house *(woss-woss)*, ironing room, and sitting room for the *houseboi*. PNG is a bit different from most tropical countries that have maids or house-girls as servants in that all the house and garden servants, even in the married quarters, are boys or men known in New Guinea Pidgin as *housebois*. The women and girls (known as *meris*) traditionally remain in the villages or the compounds, tending to their own housework—gardening, fetching water, looking after the pigs and the kids, cooking, preparing food, and generally tending to the needs of the men. The odd expatriate wife who insisted on having a *meri* as a maid soon got the message and very soon traded her in for a *houseboi*, as the *meris* were hopeless around the house.

My first *houseboi* was named Kila, and I inherited him from someone who had just left Bulolo. Kila had an old rattan chair that he had been given, and when he wasn't cleaning the house, or washing, or ironing clothes, he was relaxing in his big chair with his feet up and puffing away on a *puse*. A *puse* is a native cigarette made from locally grown tobacco leaves, rolled like a cigar, and wrapped in newspaper. It is about 15 centimetres long and shaped like a thin stick of dynamite, which is apparently where the name *puse* came from (i.e. fuse). Dynamite had long been used in the gold mining industry in PNG and especially in the Bulolo Valley.

The unfortunate thing about a native *puse* when it is in full smoke is that it stinks to high heaven, and the fumes tended to permeate up through the floorboards of the *donga*.

As someone who has never smoked, this took a bit of getting used to. Kila and I came to an amicable arrangement, however, that so long as he didn't smoke under the *donga* while I was at home, I could live with it.

One of the first PNG customs that I adopted only a couple of weeks after I arrived was to wear a *laplap*, which I bought at the local native trade store. The *laplap* is worn all over the Pacific, South, and South-East Asia, and must be the single most practical item of apparel ever invented. The *laplap*, known in various other countries as a *lavalava*, *sarong*, or *longyi*, is a simple rectangle of cotton material that is worn like a skirt by pulling one end firmly around the waist, then tucking and rolling the top down a couple of times until it is secure and won't slip down. That was in 1967, and I have worn a *laplap* (and later a *sarong*), every evening since then at home, in camps, hotels, and even once when I went to hospital.

My nearest neighbour lived in a *donga* the same as mine about 40 metres away, and we became good mates although he was away from Bulolo a lot of the time. Ebbe Mortensen was a Canadian geologist who worked for Placer Prospecting, a large Canadian mineral prospecting company. Placer operated all over PNG but was based in Bulolo. Placer Prospecting was owned by Placer Development, the parent company of CNGT, Bulolo Gold Dredging, and South Pacific Timbers. Ebbe travelled around the country with the prospecting teams, but when he was at home his favourite relaxation and entertainment was music, as was mine. Ebbe and the other geologists had bought big reel to reel tape decks, record players, and massive speakers.

Ebbe had a full set of Akai gear, which at that time was considered the best on the market.

All the stereo equipment was available from Jimmy Seeto's general store in Lae. After a couple of weeks of listening to Ebbe's music and equipment, I drove down to Lae and bought myself a record player, medium sized, but with good quality hi-fi speakers and a Toshiba reel to reel tape deck. I didn't have the sort of money that Ebbe had to spend at that time, but I bought the best gear that I could afford. I bought a few records, recorded them onto the reel to reel tapes and then swapped records with Ebbe and some of the other guys and taped these as well. In the evenings and at weekends, I just turned the reel to reel tape recorder on, loaded one of my favourite tapes, and I had music for hours without having to change records or touch the machine. I had tapes for relaxing, tapes for dancing, tapes for weekend barbecues, and tapes with romantic music necessary for those more intimate occasions when I was entertaining guests of the female persuasion.

The food at the cookhouse was good, and there was plenty of it. The cook was an Australian named Joyce, and she was a good cook. She had three *cookbois* to help her with the preparation and cleaning up, but the cooking was all done by Joyce herself. Her husband was the company cattle station manager and cowboy who looked after the cattle that CNGT grazed in the surrounding grasslands and under the young hoop pine plantations.

Bulolo was a known malarial area, so everyone took anti-malarial tablets every morning at breakfast. The tablets were supplied by the company, and there was a big jar-full on each table in the mess. The options were Nivaquin,

Chloroquin, or Camoquin. I was taking Camoquin, as that was the one recommended by my doctor before I left New Zealand. You took two tablets a day, and it was necessary to start about two weeks before arriving in PNG. There were all five major strains of human-type malaria rampant in the Bulolo Valley, but the quinine tablets were only effective against three of those. In effect, the anti-malarials we took were only a prophylactic and were not 100 percent effective against malaria; they didn't prevent you from catching it, although they did have the effect of reducing the severity of an attack.

Bulolo was a nice little town with all the amenities that a man needed: a general store-cum-grocery—which had a good range of imported Aussie tucker—a couple of banks, a post office, and a movie theatre that showed movies once a week. There was a full-length swimming pool, a hospital with an Aussie doctor and nurses, a bowling club, a golf club with a 9-hole golf course, and a church in case someone needed a wedding or a funeral. There was also a gold stamping battery which operated on an as-required basis, smelting gold from the BGD-owned sluicing claims at the Widubosh and Baiune, and the small privately owned native operations. There was one public telephone on which (when it was working) you could phone overseas, provided that you cared to pay the exorbitant toll charges.

My initial job in Bulolo was that of Roading Engineer. I was responsible for locating the road lines through the dense jungle and rugged terrain to link one logging area to the next. Once I had established a rough route for the road-line, I would survey it with an Abney Level to establish a suitable gradient for the logging trucks to traverse when fully loaded. It often meant detouring around spurs and ridge ends, and adding curves to extend the distance from one point to another. This extended distance, in effect, reduced the gradient. Once I was satisfied with the road line, my small crew cut stakes and used these to mark out the centre of the road line. I would then walk the bulldozer operators (who were all Australians at that time) over the route to gauge their opinion and the route's practicality from the construction point of view.

I usually walked the road-line with big Laurie Davis first, as he was the most experienced dozer operator and a real good bloke. Laurie usually constructed the pioneer track while Chook and Ron followed behind on their dozers, forming up the road proper. Sometimes the Department of Forest's D7 dozer, operated by Jack Haddon, would help in finishing off the roads, particularly those that were also required for Forestry Department access.

Once the grade-line was confirmed and marked, the tree fellers came in to fell all the trees on a nine metre strip to clear the road line. The extraction was then done by the bulldozers, which snigged out all the logs leaving a cleared line for Laurie with his dozer and rippers to form the pioneer track.

I had a crew of three native *bois*. These *bois* were from the Sepik River region of Papua in the south of PNG, as were most of the roading and logging crews. The term *"boi"* was a Pidgin term in general use for an adult male worker at that time. It was often combined with whatever job he did, such as *"houseboi"*, *"cookboi"*, *"tractorboi"*, etc. CNGT employed mainly Sepiks, while the Department of Forestry (which was also based in Bulolo) used mainly Chimbus from the Simbu and Wahgi Valleys in the Central Highlands of New Guinea. Sepiks are generally taller, stronger, and were considered to be more intelligent than the Chimbus. All companies and organisations had to segregate their native workers by tribe, otherwise there would be mayhem in the "coolie lines". The native housing compounds also had to be separated by tribe and with some reasonable distance between them to avoid inter-tribal confrontations, a common occurrence all over PNG.

The Art of Blowing Things Up

One of the subjects omitted from Ranger School training and from my previous experience was explosives and the art of blowing things up. I was very keen to learn how to use dynamite, but I really knew little about the subject other than watching my Dad loading his log-splitting gun with gun powder and blowing big, old, knotty pine logs apart.

As Roading Engineer, I was required to work ahead of the pioneer (rough) track-forming dozer and blast the big klinkii stumps out of the ground. Many of the trees felled along the road lines were giant klinkii pines. Most of the other species had root systems which could be torn out by the bulldozer rippers or chopped and prised out with the corner cutting edges of the dozer blade, but not the klinkii pine roots. Klinkii pines had massive tap roots which went deep down into the soil for many metres, and this made them impossible for the dozers to dig up or rip out.

My predecessor at CNGT had trained a crew of three Sepiks to dynamite stumps and handle gelignite and blasting caps, and I inherited this crew along with the job. Shortly after I started at CNGT, I was given the key to the explosives shed located out in the middle of what was known as "the rock pile". The rock pile consisted of kilometres of gold dredge tailings deposited by the action of the gold dredges. The tailings were up to 800 metres wide and covered the entire upper Bulolo Valley on either side of the river.

The explosives shed was a corrugated iron affair about 3 metres square, and it was located down inside a crater in the rock pile. The surrounding walls of rock tailings acted as a blast shield in case the dynamite ever blew up. The shed was about 100 metres from the almost-intact remains of Number Five Gold Dredge, which was the last to cease dredging operations in the Bulolo Valley when it closed in 1964.

Of course, I didn't let on to anyone that I knew nothing at all about explosives. So, on the first day that we had to blow some stumps, I got the crew together and told them to just go ahead and carry on as usual, and I would supervise operations in case they were doing something different to the way that I would do it. We collected two boxes of Semigel (a brand of dynamite), a box of blasting caps, and a couple of coils of yellow safety fuse from the explosives shed, loaded them into the back of my Jeep, and rattled off across the rock pile and into the jungle.

We collected the hand augers from the road-crew caravan (where we had our lunch and stored some equipment) and carried all our gear along the cleared road line to the first stump. We first sized up the stump and decided how many holes we needed to bore. This decision was based on the diameter of the Klinkii pine stump. A smaller stump might only require three or four holes, while a very big stump might need up to eight holes. Two of the crew operated the augers, which were about 20 centimetres in diameter, and started drilling the bore holes at approximately 45 degrees to the stump. The holes were angled so that the auger hit the tap root about 50 cm below ground level, but the auger hole was no deeper than the length of a man's arm plus a stick of dynamite. The holes were finished and cleaned out by hand.

Again, depending upon the size of the stump, we would place two to six sticks of Semigel down each hole and tamp them down firmly with a tamping pole that we had cut for the job. We then cut off a 1.8 metre length of safety fuse for each hole (it was important that all fuses were the same length so that they would detonate at the same time) and fitted a blasting cap onto one end of each length of fuse. The blasting caps had to be crimped onto the fuse. I found out much later that you are supposed to crimp the caps onto the fuse with a special crimping tool to prevent accidentally exploding the cap and blowing your hand off. My crew, however, had their own system which I didn't interfere with (not knowing any different at the time anyway), and I adopted it myself after I had watched them do it a few times without blowing off any of their appendages.

They placed the cap on a flat tree stump, poked the safety fuse up into the hollow base and then—with the back edge of their bush knife (machete), which everyone in PNG carried—they pressed down hard on the end of the cap and crimped it tightly onto the fuse. The next move was to push a sharpened stick about the size of a wooden meat skewer down into the centre of each packed-down cake of Semigel at the bottom of the drill hole, making a smaller hole. They would then gently push the blasting cap with the fuse attached into that hole and press the Semigel around the cap with their fingers to make it firm.

The crew would repeat the procedure for each auger hole, back-fill all the holes with clay, and tamp them all down tight. That left three to eight lengths of safety fuse sticking out from around the stump. Two of the crew then trotted off in opposite directions to warn anyone in the area (such as the roading crew or any wandering natives who might simply appear out of the jungle) that we were going to make a big bang and that there would be dirt and chunks of wood flying about in all directions. We also moved all our gear well away from the stump and out of harm's way.

Once we were satisfied that all was clear, members of the crew each took one or two fuse ends, lit a clump of about half a dozen matches, and on the word from me, lit all the fuses at the same time. When all fuses were fizzing away, we shouted out a final warning to the world at large and took to our heels to get as far away from the action as possible.

That thundering WHOOOOMP, and the sight of a huge cloud of dirt and smoke and bits of stump heading skywards was always a satisfying spectacle and indicated another job well done. I loved blowing things up!

One day I rediscovered a very big klinkii stump, which I hadn't blasted previously because I reckoned it was far enough off the road-line not to be a problem. We needed to do a slight road realignment on a bend, however, and the forming-up dozers needed to cut an extra few metres off a bank to get the batter right. This brought the big stump into the road-line, so it had to be removed.

The interesting thing about this stump was that it already had a 15 centimetre diameter hole down the centre. The hole went about 1.5 metres down into the tap root. I reckoned it would need about ten auger holes to blow this beast, all drilled by hand. So after due consideration I had a brainwave: "Why not save some effort and blow it up from the inside?"

I got the crew to fill the bottom half of the hole with clay so that it was then only about 80 centimetres deep. Then I packed about 20 sticks of Semigel down the hole. The crew looked a bit worried about the use of so much dynamite, as we hadn't tried this trick before. Anyway, we got the blasting cap and fuse down into the hole and packed the rest of it up to the top with more clay.

The roading crew had a steel four-wheeled caravan that they towed with one of the bulldozers to keep it close to the roading operations for convenient access during lunch and smoko breaks. When we had left the camp in the morning, the caravan had been parked about 250 metres away through the bush, and the bulldozers were working a similar distance away. Unbeknown to us, however, Laurie had decided to tow the caravan up to where they were about to start on the new cut and had parked it just below the bank less than 40 metres away from the high ground where we were about to blast. We had shouted out the usual warnings, but apparently the road crew hadn't heard because they were directly below us and the dozer engines were running at the time. By the time we messed around deciding which way we were going to run and had lit a single, rather longer fuse than usual, the roading crew had knocked off for smoko.

The roading crew *bois* who worked with the dozers had settled around the fire to eat their *kaukau* (sweet potato) on the far side of the caravan. Three of the dozer operators had already gone into the caravan, and Laurie was standing in the doorway at the top of the steps, kicking mud off his boots, when the stump went up.

The stump blew into a few million splinters, which showered all over the bush leaving a massive hole in the ground. Total success—from the demolition point of view, anyway.

Because of the enclosed, hard casing of the stump around the dynamite and the excessive amount of explosive that I had used, the bang was so loud and sharp that it sounded like a bomb going off. It was heard as far away as Bulolo township!

The roading crew's caravan was a steel shell with no lining. When the shockwave hit, it must have been like being inside an empty drum with someone pounding the outside with a sledgehammer.

The roading crew *bois* outside by the fire hit the ground in terror. Chook, Jack, and Ron in the caravan fell off their seats and banged their appendages on various projections, while poor old Laurie, who was still standing in the doorway, whipped his head up and cracked it on the steel door frame, resulting in a decent cut to his head with blood pouring everywhere.

For some reason, I was *persona non grata* around the roading crew for a few days. "That bloody 'Kayway' [that's 'Kiwi' in Orstralian], I'll kill the bastard!" was the consensus of the day. I thought it wise to lie low for a bit after that, so I found some urgent work that needed doing on the other side of the forest.

One day when I was doing an audit of our explosives stock in the dynamite shed on the rock pile, I discovered that about half of the one hundred or so boxes of Semigel were so old that much of it had liquefied inside the waxed, waterproof boxes, and the liquid nitro-glycerine was slopping around in the bottom. One thing that I had learned was that when dynamite became liquid like that, it was extremely volatile; if banged or dropped it was very likely to explode.

I rounded up my trusty stump blasting crew, and we opened up all the boxes of Semigel that were in the store. We very carefully sorted the sticks and put all the good, sound dynamite into boxes on one side of the shed, and all the liquefied and unstable-looking stuff on the other. Once we had completed the sorting, I got the crew to carefully carry the liquid and unstable Semigel, one box at a time, along a track through the rock pile to a protected crater that I had picked out about 100 metres away and stack the stuff carefully in a heap. I very circumspectly hung back and "supervised" this part of the operation from a respectable distance, because if one of the *bois* had tripped over while carrying a box of liquid nitro then he, and anyone nearby, would have been blown to kingdom come in the resulting explosion.

Fortunately, they managed to get all the boxes into a heap at the bottom of the crater without mishap. I then took one sound stick of Semigel from the good stuff, a blasting cap, and a length of safety fuse, and carefully placed the charged stick amongst the dodgy boxes. The fuse was lit, and we all took to our scrapers like rats up a drainpipe! The location of my mound of liquid TNT in the rock pile was about 1.5 kilometres from Bulolo town centre, but the resultant explosion rattled all the windows, terrified the inhabitants, and the local natives thought that the "Japs" had returned to finish off what they had started in 1942. There were more mutterings from the Ockers about that "bloody Kayway", but by this time they had already decided that I was some sort of a lunatic, and they just had to learn to live with me.

Finding my Feet

Not long after I arrived in Bulolo, I bought myself a 1962 Holden sedan. It was a good vehicle for the PNG gravelled roads, but it couldn't travel off-road into the bush, through the mud, or along the dirt bush tracks, as it didn't have four-wheel drive. So, when one of the company mechanics, Laurie Whitting, asked if I wanted to go out in his four-wheel drive Jeep one Sunday morning to the New Tribes Mission Station over the Watut River on the border of Kukukuku country, I jumped at the opportunity.

PNG is festooned with mission stations of various religious persuasions, all trying to save the souls of the natives. Some of them did actually achieve the odd bit of useful stuff in some of the native villages by providing medical services and education. The mission out at the Watut was a New Tribes Mission, which was an American missionary organisation representing mixed Protestant (mainly Baptist) denominations, and originating out of the Bible Belt of the southern United States. Although most staff members at the New Tribes were American, there were also a handful of Australians and New Zealanders in the mix.

I was told that there was a Kiwi family at the Watut Mission Station and I was keen to meet them. The head of the mission was an Italian-American named Tuss Tucelli, who had been a dentist back in the States. When anyone in Bulolo contracted dental problems, they either suffered and got it fixed when they went back to Australia on leave, or braved the one and a half hour trip along a four-wheel drive track out to the Watut Mission Station to see Tuss. There were three couples who were resident at the mission; Tuss and his wife Eleanor, Dan and Corinne Palmer, and Ike and Mary Samuels from New Zealand. There were also two single American women. The latter were in their thirties and rather plain looking, which I guessed was why they had possibly given up on their marriage prospects and were hiding out in the New Guinea jungle.

Anyway, five of us piled into Laurie's Willys Jeep and headed out over the CNGT logging roads, through the Klinkii pine forest, over the Bulolo-Watut range, down into the Watut Valley to the river, and across the bridge over the Watut River near the Golden Pines sawmill. Golden Pines was a small private sawmilling company that was logging on the Watut side of the river, sawing all their logs, and then trucking the sawn timber down to Lae for export. Once across the river, we turned left and carried on up the south side of the river on a dirt track towards the mission station.

After crossing the Bulolo ridge I had started to feel pretty crook, first with nausea, then alternatively with hot sweats, fever, and cold shivers. I got Laurie to stop a couple of times, after we had crossed the river, so I could throw up. Then I became so hot that I felt like I was burning up, and I had to lie down in a creek that ran alongside the track to try to cool down.

The closer we got to the mission station, the sicker I got. I had no idea what was wrong with me. The boys reckoned that I probably had a bad hangover from too much SP beer (South Pacific Lager) at the Golf Club the night before, but I had never had a hangover like this.

By the time we reached the mission, I was delirious and in quite a bad way. The guys carried me up to Ike's house and plonked me on an old sofa on the verandah. Ike took one look at me and immediately diagnosed malaria. He went straight to his kerosene fridge and got out his medical gear. He gave me an injection to stop the vomiting, and a quinine shot to kill the malaria, and then put me to bed in his spare room. I don't remember anything about that first day at the mission or much about the next couple of days, during which Ike followed up with more anti-malarial shots. The other guys returned to Bulolo on the Sunday afternoon and left me at Ike's place. I started to come right after three or four days, although I was as weak as a kitten.

On the Thursday, Tuss gave me a ride back to Bulolo in his old Land Cruiser. I reported to the boss and was told to take the week off and get plenty of rest to recover from the effects of the fever. It turned out that I had contracted vivax malaria, which was the most common form in the Bulolo area. Two weeks later I was as right as rain and back at work again. Malaria can knock the stuffing out of you though, and it does take a while before you are back operating on all cylinders.

After I traded my Holden in for a Land Rover, my mate Jim Riley and I would often drive out to the mission station on a weekend, and we became good friends with Ike, Tuss, and the others. Jim and I were interested in the work they were doing in the area, particularly their relationship with the Watut and the Kukukuku people.

Jim was a Kiwi from Thames and one of the three New Zealanders living in Bulolo. He was an ex-NZFS Forest Ranger from the intake two years before mine. He lived up on the hill in the PNG Department of Forests compound and was an instructor at the Bulolo Forest Ranger School. Jim and I became good mates, particularly as we had similar backgrounds and interests in ethnology, cannibals, forestry, girls, beer, boats, fishing, hunting, guns, and Land Rovers (not necessarily in that order), and we spent many of our weekends doing stuff together.

I had my Land Rover painted a bright lime green by one of the mechanics at the forestry workshops on a "mate's rates" basis. Jim had a blue short wheel-base Land Rover of similar vintage and model to mine.

When I first met him, Jim had lived with Ross Wylie, another Forestry School instructor in a Forestry Department *donga* up the hill from the company part of town. At one stage, both Ross and Jim contracted malaria within a day of each other, and they were both very sick puppies for a few weeks. According to the Aussie doctor at the Bulolo Hospital, they had caught cerebral malaria, which was the worst and most dangerous of all the types you could get in PNG. It could seriously affect the brain if not treated aggressively and immediately. Fortunately, the Bulolo Hospital had all the good stuff needed to cure malaria, and the doctor was very skilled in treating the disease, so they eventually came right without any long-term effects.

When Ross married his Australian fiancée Pat, who then moved to Bulolo, Jim moved into his own *donga* and started cooking for himself. I decided to stop eating at the cookhouse and joined up with him by sharing the cost of the food, and cooking and eating the evening meal up at his place three or four nights a week. He had a proper kitchen and all the gear, while mine was a more basic affair, although sufficiently well-equipped and functional enough to make my own meals when I wasn't eating up at Jim's.

There was a good swimming hole a few kilometres down the Lae road from Bulolo on the Baiune River below the old BGD power station that still powered the nearby BGD gold sluicing operations. Sometimes on a Sunday, Ron and Laurie from the workshop, and Jim and I would round up a bunch of Bulolo residents and drive out to the river in a convoy for a swim and a picnic. We would pack up the picnic lunches and the chilly bins of beer and head for the Baiune for the day, taking lilos and inflated truck tubes with us to raft down the rapids. We rigged up a rope swing from a tree, so we could swing out from the bank and drop into the pool. There was a dozen or so *papaya* (pawpaw) trees hanging off the river bank near the hole, and we were always able to collect plenty of fresh papaya to eat.

Bulolo had a nine-hole golf course with two separate tees on each hole to make up eighteen holes. I had never picked up a golf club in my life, but Laurie Davis and others persuaded me to give it a try. I had already become a member, as the golf club was a popular place to have a beer on a Saturday afternoon after work (we worked five and a half days a week), and the beer was cheaper there than at the Pine Lodge Hotel on the hill. So I borrowed some clubs, and Laurie and Troutie Russell (the thinnings foreman) took it upon themselves to teach me the finer points of the gentleman's game. I picked up the basics reasonably quickly and started to enjoy my weekly round, improving as I went.

The golf club and the bowling club were the main drinking spots for the CNGT and Forestry guys, and they were also the venues for concerts and dances from time to time. In addition to the Aussie barmaids up at the Pine Lodge Hotel, a couple of nurses and a school teacher, some of the families who worked for CNGT and the Department of Forests possessed a gaggle of older teenage daughters who attended boarding school in Australia. These girls usually came home to Bulolo during school holidays and at Christmas. They were a sociable lot, and most of them were keen to accompany us on our numerous excursions and picnics to the rivers, villages, and various other places of interest. Some of these girls returned to Bulolo when they finished school and got jobs at CNGT, the Forestry Department, and in the stores and banks in town.

One concert was organised by a bunch of the ladies headed by one called Lovie, who was always organising something. It was to be a Kasbah night, and Jim and I were asked to put on a Kiwi act. We decided to dress up as Maori, wearing grass-skirts and gumboots and with bare chests and face *moko* (tattoos). The "tattoos" were done on the afternoon of the concert by Barbara (her father was a shift foreman at the ply mill) and Sue (daughter of the log loader operator), using their eyebrow liner and whatever other makeup they could find.

They used a picture of a Maori moko that Jim found as a guide, and they did a really good job. Our act needed a couple of Maori maidens to complete the troupe, so we roped in Barbara and Sue with their Trobriand Island grass skirts, and they made their own tops to complete the look. I played the accompaniment on my guitar, and Jim and I sang Peter Cape's "Down the Hall on Saturday Night" (hence the need for gumboots) and "Taumarunui on the Main Trunk Line". We had taught Sue and Barb the words of the Maori favourites "Pokarekare Ana" and "Hoki Mai", so all four of us sang those songs to my accompaniment on the guitar. Our performance was enthusiastically received by the predominantly Aussie audience, and we were considered one of the star acts of the night.

Trouble at the Pine Lodge Hotel

The Pine Lodge Hotel stood on the hill above Bulolo town. It not only served the good South Pacific Lager known as SP, but also employed a seemingly endless supply of Aussie barmaids. At one side of the hotel were the barmaids' quarters, some accommodation for guests, and the house of the publican, Ted Ferry.

The hotel had three bars. The main bar, located at the front, was a comfortable lounge bar with a long bar, and rattan chairs and tables. This bar was for expats and visitors only.

Out the back of the Hotel was the *Boi* Bar. This was for native men only (no expats or women allowed) and consisted of a three-sided concrete floored and walled structure with a concrete ledge around the sides as a substitute for tables. The serving area was also concrete but designed so that there was only enough space for the barmaid to take the money and pass the bottles of SP through to the *bois* in the bar.

The third bar was a small verandah tacked onto the side of the hotel on the same side as the barmaids' quarters. This had wooden seats and a couple of tables, and there was enough space for about a dozen drinkers. This was generally known as the bachelors' or single expats' bar, although we single guys were also permitted to drink in the main lounge bar if we so desired.

The *Boi* Bar was luxuriously fitted out in concrete for a good reason. On native pay-day, which was Friday night, the *bois* would pour into the *Boi* Bar to drink up large. There were Chimbus from the Forestry Department labour gangs, Sepiks from the CNGT company compounds, and a few Buangs, Watuts, and people from other tribes who happened to be around town at the time. When they first arrived, everyone was friendly enough, just generally talking and recounting events of the past week. After the first bottle of SP had been consumed, the conversations got a little bit louder. After the second bottle, a few minor arguments broke out, and the shouting began. After the third bottle, the whole mob became as pissed as chooks, and all hell broke loose! Bottles were thrown, smashed, and used as weapons. Punches were thrown, men were vomiting and bleeding, and the fighting got totally out of control. It was bedlam! Ted, or one of the girls, would phone the police station for the riot boys who were on standby and expecting trouble because the same thing happened every pay night.

The police, who were Tolais from Rabaul on New Britain Island, soon arrived with their paddy wagon and with their riot shields and batons at the ready. Although the revellers in the *Boi* Bar were of various tribal groups, there were never any Tolais amongst them, so the Tolai policemen got stuck in with plenty of enthusiasm. Batons were wielded with great gusto, heads cracked, noses broken, and blood and vomit spread everywhere. Then the cops shovelled the bodies out into the paddy wagon. Once the wagon was full, they would race up to the Police Station, pour them out into the cells, and charge back for another load. Eventually all was quiet, the entertainment was over, the cops went back to the station, and we ordered another beer.

Now was the time for Ted's native staff to couple up the high-pressure hoses, open the grate to the pit at the end of the *Boi* Bar, and proceed to hose down the entire interior including ceiling, walls, and floor. They then sluiced the glass, vomit, blood, teeth, and who knows what else down the conveniently located drains and into the cess pit. Within half an hour, all was flushed clean again and ready for the next night. An efficient system indeed!

Sometimes I would take my guitar up to the verandah bar of a Saturday evening, and the bachelor boys, the school teachers and nurses (who were all of the female persuasion), would park themselves around the verandah, order a few beers, and have a sing-song. We would drink and sing until we got chucked out at the ten-thirty closing time.

Ted occasionally came out to remind me that it was ok to play the guitar and sing out there on the verandah, but that we must keep the volume down when there were natives drinking in the *Boi* Bar. We weren't allowed to sing at all on pay nights when the mob came in. The problem was that music of any kind indicated to the natives that a *sing-sing* celebration (traditional native dancing and singing) was in the offing and, after one or two SPs, the music would set them off. They would go wild, and the fighting would begin.

One Saturday night we didn't think there were many *bois* out the back drinking, as they had had a fairly heavy session the previous evening. There was quite a crowd of us on the verandah, and we felt like a party, so I got started with the guitar, and everyone got singing. Well, we got a bit happier and a bit louder, then a lot happier and a lot louder, and then all hell broke loose out the back! Apparently, there was quite a large mob out back in the *Boi* Bar, and the singing and the guitar playing had started them off good and proper.

A riot soon got under way, and the Tolai cops arrived and suggested that we get out and go home before the *bois* moved around to the verandah. At this point, Ted Ferry marched out and told me in no uncertain terms that I was banned for life from the Pine Lodge Hotel with immediate effect.

For the next six weeks, I drank at the Bowling Club or the Golf Club, as did my mates. Old Ted started to notice the drop in his takings. Our friendly barmaids made sure that Ted got the message and suggested to him that he should let me back into the hotel again. Ted didn't want to lose face, so he told one of the girls to suggest to me that I could start drinking on the verandah again, but only so long as I didn't bring my guitar. A bunch of us duly appeared back on the verandah one Saturday night, and all was sunshine and roses—for a while anyway. That "life sentence" had lasted six weeks.

But rehabilitation doesn't last forever, and some months later it was someone's birthday; the guitar came out again and away we went, singing and drinking and having a good time. It was all right for a couple of hours until a riot started out the back, and I got banned for life yet again. Such is life.

The second life ban lasted about two months, and then we were back again. Actually, Ted went on leave to Australia, and we moved back in while he was away. The acting manager in his absence also happened to be the senior barmaid who was one of my very (as in "very, very") close friends at the time, and she extended me a personal invitation.

Fireworks at Wau

Jim and I wandered about the New Guinea countryside and into the jungle at any opportunity, visiting villages, mission stations, gold sluicing operations, the old gold dredges, and anything else that looked interesting. We would often drive up the Bulolo Valley to Wau. It was only 30 kilometres, but it took us an hour to get there as the road was badly gravelled, pot-holed, windy, and narrow. The world-renowned Bernice P. Bishop Natural History Museum headquartered in Honolulu, Hawaii, had a collection and research station based in Wau.

Jim and I became mates with two of the resident scientists, and we often threw a few cold SPs into the Land Rover and went up to spend a Sunday with them; Phil Colman and Peter Shanahan were both Aussies, and they were real good blokes.

Phil was a malacologist (snails and shells specialist) from Sydney, and Peter was a small animal expert. They had a team of local New Guineans working for them on the collection side, and other scientists from Honolulu would visit on short-term projects. Their work was very interesting, and Jim and I enjoyed catching up on their latest finds, observations, and discoveries when we went up to Wau.

Phil and Peter had a collection of live animals and birds that they were studying, and this changed or was added to on a regular basis. They had this huge pet python, which we used to carry about and wrap around ourselves. It was sixteen feet long, weighed sixty pounds, and was as thick as a man's leg. They also had a pygmy possum, sugar gliders, a *cuscus* (a tree climbing kangaroo, which looks like a large golden possum), and a big Papuan hornbill known locally as a "woosh-woosh bird" or *kokomo*.

The woosh-woosh bird's name denotes the sound made by its wings as it flies through the jungle among the tree tops. The one at Phil and Peter's house was a pet they had raised from a chick. It was about 130 centimetres long, with a 150 centimetre wingspan, and it had an enormous hooked beak. It was the most comical looking bird I had ever seen.

We would often sit on the steps of the old house where they lived, drinking SP, and catching up on the local gossip. The *kokomo* would hear us from somewhere in the depths of the house and come hopping out in its most peculiar way, which was a bit like a wallaby leaping along. It would park itself on the top step and stare at us with one beady red eye and its head cocked to one side and wait. Peter usually had a big jar of ripe red coffee beans at hand, and he would throw one up to the bird, which would catch it neatly with the tip of its long beak, flick it back, and swallow it. Then we would start the count-down, and before we could count to a hundred—plop—the coffee bean, minus its outer red coating, would drop out of the bird's rear-end onto the floor. This trick would be repeated ad nauseam until either the bird got bored and hopped off somewhere else or we ran out of beer or coffee beans. This, of course, was all done in the cause of science. We concluded that the *kokomo* had a straight pipe with no baffles.

Wau was an interesting place. It had an airfield that was built on a hillside on a fairly steep slope. This was an important airfield during the Second World War, and there were many battles between the Japs and the Aussies to try to keep or wrest control of it. It was located roughly in the middle of the Kokoda Trail between Port Moresby on the southern coast and Salamaua on the northern coast, so it was a critical supply point for the defending troops. The old corrugated iron shed on the western side of the airstrip was the original terminal building, and it was still full of bullet and shrapnel holes when I was there.

The surrounding area, particularly on the eastern side of the airstrip, was all in scrub and low bush, and the Department of Forests decided in its wisdom to clear it and plant it with hoop pine. It consisted of a few hundred acres of rough land, and they brought up a gang of Chimbus from Bulolo to hand-cut the taller scrub and create a source of dry fuel to carry a fire through the entire area so as to prepare it for tree planting.

The day came when the cut scrub had dried sufficiently and conditions were considered just right for a good burn-off. The Forestry guys positioned about fifty Chimbus around the perimeter of the cut area. At the signal, they struck their matches and lit their fires. The breeze was good, and soon more than a hundred fires took hold then joined up, and the burn started to move toward the centre.

Then…bang, bang, BOOM! It sounded like a war had started up. There were bullets and shrapnel flying everywhere! The Chimbus and the Forestry guys hit the turf, trying to find something to hide behind, and dived for cover, but the battle just kept raging.

The Forestry Department hadn't done their homework—that area was vacant, scrub covered, and with no native gardens for a good reason. The locals all knew that it was covered in abandoned ammunition from when the war ended! Much of it had been buried under only a few centimetres of soil, and some of it was practically on the surface, covered by years of scrub and weeds. A lot of it was scattered individual rounds, but there were also cases of cartridges, as well as hand grenades, a few anti-aircraft shells, and various other explosives. The fire was totally out of control by this time, and there were more explosions, and metal and lead flying everywhere each time the fire front found more ammo.

The terrified Chimbus crawled away on their bellies into the surrounding jungle, and it was days before some of them were found and taken back to their compound at Bulolo. It was two days before many of the residents of Wau and the villages located near the airstrip ventured back to their homes. Miraculously, no-one was killed, although bullets and shrapnel were found buried in walls around Wau for quite a while.

Cannibals!

The Kukukukus command a huge jungle territory in the highlands of the Morobe District of New Guinea. Their western boundary starts near Garaina, south west of Wau and close to the northern border of the Northern District, and their territory expands all the way east to Menyamya and Yandabome near the border of the Eastern Highlands. The main villages of the Kukukuku are Aseki, which is south of Wau on the western side, and Menyamya in the east.

As I have mentioned, the Kukukukus are small in stature but are feared by all other tribes as fierce warriors, headhunters, and cannibals. Most Kukukuku men carry a star-shaped stone club with a ninety-centimetre-long hardwood handle, and a bow and arrows, and they usually wear a bark cloak, which is unique to the Kukukuku people. The bark cloaks are used to protect them from the rain, but also as a disguise when stalking the enemy, as the Kukukuku men will crouch down behind a tree under their bark cloaks and become practically invisible. The cloak is also folded, tucked into a string belt, and hung down behind them like half a skirt to protect them from arrows fired from behind.

The Kukukuku *meris* also wear the bark cape and always have a *bilum* bag hanging from their heads. *Bilums* are woven from grey or coloured string that the *meris* make by rolling bark fibres on their thighs until they have long lengths of a strong but thin twine. The string is then mixed with wood ash. The *bilums* might contain a baby, a piglet, *kaukau*, or all of the above.

By the time I settled in PNG, some of the Kukukuku villages—mainly around the northern perimeter of the territory—had been visited by the *Kiaps* and missionaries, and as a result some limited form of contact had developed with the outside world.

Some Kukukukus brought out produce from their gardens and the jungle to trade for salt, tobacco, and other items that they could then trade on with the more isolated Kukukuku groups and villages of the interior. The main border contact points at that time were the New Tribes Mission at the Watut, a market near the Golden Pines bridge over the Watut River, and another market near the edge of Wau. Natives of other tribes never ventured into Kukukuku territory to trade or for any other reason—unless they were carried in, feet first!

Jim and I would sometimes go up to Wau on a weekend, call in and see the boys at the Bishop Museum, and then visit the Kukukuku market on the edge of town. Some of the Bulolo and Wau expatriates and the local natives would go to the market to buy fresh vegetables and smoked bush meat. The vegetables were fresh and varied, and included *kaukau* of many varieties (the staple diet of the New Guinea native), beans of various sizes and types (including the giant bean, which is about ninety centimetres long and five to eight centimetres wide), tomatoes, and various other produce.

The smoked bush meat was particularly tasty and there was a steady demand for it, although mainly by the local natives. The animals were all caught, shot, or trapped deep in the jungle, cut into strips, and smoked over green leaves and twigs near the spot where they were killed.

The meat included cassowary (a jungle emu), bush wallaby, *cuscus*, wild pig, and various birds. It was not always easy to establish exactly what you were buying because all smoked bush meat looks much the same. It is a yellow colour, smells strongly of smoke, and is cut into regular-sized strips. As buyers, we had to rely on the Kukukuku *meris* at the market to tell us what we were buying. The problem with this was that, firstly, we expat buyers weren't fluent in the Kukukuku *Tok Pisin* (Pidgin) and, secondly, the meat had been killed by hunters far in the interior and had probably been traded numerous times before it reached the market at Wau. Sometimes they got the identification right, but other times it could be something entirely different. I would buy the occasional piece of meat from the market, particularly the wild pork and cassowary, which I enjoyed, and I would also buy some for my *houseboi* to take home to his family. The meat was easy to prepare when I was cooking for myself, as it was already almost pre-cooked by the smoking process, so it just needed slicing up, mixing with vegetables, and heating up in a pan.

One day in 1969, after I had been buying and eating Kukukuku smoked bush meat off and on for a couple of years, some government health people who were visiting Wau decided to collect samples of bush meat from the Kukukuku market and take it for testing. A couple of months later I received a call, on the quiet, from Dave Dixon, the local Police Inspector. He said that he had been advised of certain concerns by the health department people in Port Moresby, who had received the results of the Wau bush meat tests. Apparently, they had identified a number of different species amongst the meat samples collected from the market, including cassowary, wallaby, flying fox, *cuscus*, wild pig, and...*Homo sapiens!*

Further investigations and tests of more samples followed, and some months later they confirmed what had originally been suspected; some of the bush meat that the Kukukuku traders at the Wau market had been selling had been positively identified as human meat. Cannibalism was still known to be widely carried out in the interior of PNG, particularly by the Kukukuku, and the common method of preparation for "long pig" (as the early NZ Maori called cooked missionary) was to cut it into strips and smoke it before storing it for later consumption or trading it on. That is, of course, the same preservation method that was used for pork, cassowary, wallaby, and the other bush meat that we were buying. For some time (and no-one knows for how long it had been going on), bush pork, and "long pig" had been sold side by side at the Wau market. Apparently bush pig and "long pig" taste very similar, at least according to all the cannibals that I have ever met anyway.

The question for the government was whether to make the findings public and create a furore or just shut up, stop the sale of bush meat at the Wau market, and hope that not too many people found out about it. In the end, after considerable gnashing of teeth in certain government circles, the latter course of action was decided upon. So, although a few of us were in the know, this rather controversial bit of information was kept away from the general public.

The 64,000-dollar question remains: how much, if any, "long pig" had I and my friends unknowingly consumed over the previous couple of years? We will never know, of course, but the chances are about even that I may have eaten the odd select cut of someone's relation in the belief that it was, in fact, "short pig".

Killers in Bark Capes

I found the Kukukuku a fascinating people with an ancient and interesting culture that I wanted to learn more about, so living on the borders of Kukukuku country was a great opportunity to further my interest in primitive cultures. One of the best places to start was the New Tribes Mission at the Watut, so I would visit there whenever I had the opportunity, especially to spend time with Ike Samuels.

Ike was a New Zealand Maori from the Rotorua area who, with his wife, had joined the New Tribes Mission some years before, establishing themselves at the Watut.

The mission was located just inside the boundaries of Kukukuku territory, and the upper Watut people who lived around the mission are a sub-tribe of the Kukukuku. The Watuts, in fact, objected to being called Kukukuku, which was fine by us. We were more than happy to call them whatever they liked!

The Kukukuku people are very isolated and had little to do with other tribes unless they were trying to kill and eat them. In fact, Kukukuku tribesmen were known in PNG as the "Killers in Bark Capes". The only access into or across their territory was on foot over jungle trails. Therefore, other than the Watut who lived near the mission station and the few villagers located near the borders of their territory, the Kukukuku did not generally speak Pidgin. They spoke only their own tribal language, which is called Kapau.

Learning or understanding Kapau is extremely difficult for English speakers, mainly because the language comprises many glottal stops. Glottal stops are sounds made in the epiglottis, or deep in the throat, and can be compared somewhat to the "click" language of the Xhosa people of South Africa (except that Xhosa clicks are made with the tongue against the palate). Despite this, Ike had learned to speak basic Kapau over many years and had hand-written a Kapau-Pidgin dictionary. Ike's dictionary was very difficult to understand, and although I did learn a few words, Ike's dots and dashes mixed with letters were not easy to decipher unless you were hearing the Kapau language used every day.

I made numerous trips into Kukukuku country with Ike. The nearest Kukukuku village to the mission was about a two-hour trek through the *kunai* grass-covered hills and jungle from the Watut mission. It was called Patangkahau. The villagers had become used to seeing Ike and the missionaries, and eventually they also accepted me.

In 1968, on a long holiday weekend, I accompanied Ike on a three-day trip deep into Kukukuku territory where he had been given permission to witness a Kukukuku initiation and nose-piercing ceremony.

The Kukukuku men, like most Highland tribes in PNG, wore bones through their noses, and often also in their ears. The bones (usually pig tusks, dog teeth or cassowary bones) were forced through the septum of the nose of young boys at about age thirteen or fourteen, and this was a major step to them becoming a men and warriors.

The nose-piercing and initiation ceremonies of the Kukukuku, however, had always been a mystery, shrouded in secrecy and spiritual significance, and had never been seen by any outsider before. Ike had been working with one particular group of Kukukuku in the interior for about two years and had befriended the local chief, a man named Ninka. At long last, Ike had been invited to attend a nose-piercing ceremony where two boys were about to be initiated into the tribe. As initiated youths, these boys would then move into the men's houses, which were separate from the houses in which the *meris* and *pikininis* lived. Ike obtained approval from Ninka to let me accompany him.

The nose piercing ceremony is a major event in the life of every Kukukuku boy and takes place over a period of four days. Ike had secured the use of an eight millimetre movie camera belonging to the mission. Ike, Ninka, and I, with four Kukukuku tribesmen who had come down from the interior to act as our guides, left the mission an hour before daylight on the Saturday morning. We walked over obscure jungle trails all day and finally arrived at Ninka's village late in the evening.

We ate with the villagers that night and slept on low rattan racks in a round grass hut with a fire smouldering in the centre. The fire burned and smoked all night to keep the mosquitoes at bay.

The two boys that were to be initiated had been kept in a small grass hut, hidden out in the bush under the guard of about a dozen Kukukuku tribesmen for five days. They were not allowed to eat or to be seen by or have contact with women at any time during this period.

Early the next morning, Ike and I were led by six Kukukukus into the jungle and up onto a ridge considered by the villagers to be a magical and auspicious place where the spirits lived. On this ridge were a dozen high towers built from poles, and at the top of each of these towers was a warrior swinging a long rattan wand around and around.

The whining, howling sound made by these whirling wands sent shivers up my spine; this humming, whirring, howling, roaring sound echoed around the hills and through the jungle. These warriors had been swinging these roarers since the sun came up with the purpose of keeping the *tambarans* (spirits) at bay while the ceremony was being performed. It was an incredibly primitive sound that contributed to the eeriness and spiritual feeling of the whole place.

Soon after we arrived, two lines of Kukukukus appeared out of the jungle with a pair of men physically supporting each of the two young initiates, who were obviously weak from hunger. The columns of warriors accompanying the initiates were flailing at the boys with leaves and branches as they were dragged along. The leaf and branch slapping was to keep the *tambarans* away from the initiates.

The men supporting the boys had one hand clamped over the mouth and nose of each initiate as they approached. The boys were led to a chosen spot where they sat on the ground. They were surrounded by their entourage, which still waved branches at them, and the tribesmen whirled their *tambaran* scarers up in the towers to maintain the eerie howling and roaring.

The *Sanguma* (witch doctor) then approached the boys and produced two bones which looked like pig tusks or long dog's teeth, sharpened at each end. A man stood on either side of each initiate and held him firmly while the *Sanguma*, who was chanting and wailing, approached the first boy. He bent down and forced a bone through the septum of the boy's nose. This must have hurt like hell, as the expression on the initiate's face indicated excruciating pain! He didn't cry out, however, because to do so would have shown cowardice, and he would have been seen as unfit to become a man and a warrior.

The *Sanguma* then approached the second initiate, who had been staring straight ahead all this time. He forced the second bone straight through the septum of the second boy's nose as he had done with the first initiate. Neither boy visibly flinched or cried out, but the pain on their faces was difficult to watch. Eventually, after a lot more chanting and calling to the spirits, the entire group surrounded the now- initiated young warriors, moved slowly back down the hill, and returned to the village to continue with the ceremony.

Once back in the village, the tribe commenced with the mass slaughter of about 100 pigs, and many Kukukukus from neighbouring villages began to arrive to join the festivities. The initiates were given the first pork to eat as it came off the fires, after which everyone else joined in the feast. This was an incredible experience for me and one I will never forget.

Ross on an elephant in Myanmar, formerly known as Burma. A person would sit in the basket behind the driver.

ROSS LOCKYER –
LOGGING ADVENTURER

GET OUT YOUR WORLD MAP AND SETTLE DOWN FOR A STORY OF ADVENTURE, DISCOVERY, AND INGENUITY AS WE TALK TO KERIKERI'S ROSS LOCKYER ABOUT HIS FASCINATING CAREER IN FORESTRY.

The article that appeared in *New Zealand Logger* magazine (May 2006 edition). My rediscovery of this article prompted me to start writing.

The virtually intact remains of the No. 5 (rear) and No. 7 gold dredges in the Bulolo Valley as I found them in 1967.

My first company vehicle, a 1942, ex-US army Willys Jeep. Bulolo, 1967.

Kila (at right) with his *houseboi* mates outside my *donga*, Bulolo, 1967.

At home in Bulolo, 1967, wearing a *laplap*, which has been my standard item of clothing ever since for relaxing in the evenings.

Gold sluicing at the Widubosh, Bulolo Valley, 1968.

CNGT logging truck with a load of klinkii pine logs bound for the plymill at
Bulolo. Main Watut – Bulolo forestry road, 1970.

Jim, Barbara, Sue and me at the Kasbah Night, Bulolo, 1969. We were a star act!

The Department of Forests' *lik-lik* doctor, Peter Woolcott,
and his pet *kokomo*. Bulolo, 1968.

A Kukukuku headhunter and cannibal, first time out of the jungle, meets me, his first white man. Ike Samuels' house, New Tribes Mission, Watut, 1968.

Watut *meris* and *pikininis*, Patangkahau Village, Watut Valley, 1967.

Kukukuku tribesmen, known as the "Killers in Bark Capes", arriving in the Watut forestry area for the planned filming of "Forest Without Spears". Watut, 1970.

Kukukuku tribesmen simulating an attack on an enemy village for the filming of "Forest Without Spears". Upper Watut, 1970.

Kukukuku initiation ceremony. Bone being forced through the nose of the first initiate. Kukukuku territory, 1968.

A second Kukukuku initiate has his nose pierced as part of an initiation ceremony. Kukukuku territory, 1968.

Kukuku headhunter armed for battle, Watut Valley, 1970. Simulates an intertribal battle for the film shoot of "Forest Without Spears".

Kukukuku headhunter with his killing club. Encountered deep in Kukukuku country, 1968

Bush Boss

In 1968, Pappy Burmeister resigned from the position of Logging Foreman and returned to Australia. Pappy had been in charge of logging operations since before I arrived in PNG, and now I was promoted to the position of Bush Boss in his place—in charge of all forestry operations, including logging, thinning, and roading for CNGT.

The company provided me with a new, red, four-wheel drive International Harvester ute (utility truck) with a canopy and bench seats at the back. It was fitted with a VHF radio so that I could communicate with the company office back in Bulolo. We installed another mobile VHF unit at the logging camp smoko hut in case of an accident in the bush. I was now supervising three separate operations—roading, logging, and production thinning operations—as well as collecting spare parts, arranging for repairs, keeping in touch with the office, and handling production records and administration.

I had a felling crew of eight Sepiks, of which the two top men were Kinoi, the *boss-boi*, and his deputy, Arto. They had been with CNGT for many years. They were intelligent and as skilled at their job as any tree fellers that I have seen anywhere.

The huge klinkii pine trees (some as tall as 85 metres), were dead straight, perfectly balanced, and often difficult to fell directionally. The trees needed first to be scarfed with a deep scarf facing the direction in which the tree was required to fall. Once the tree had been partially back-cut, steel wedges were driven in with a sledge hammer to tip the tree in the desired direction.

The log extraction (snigging) was done by three bulldozers equipped with winches. These were operated by Australians at that time. The yarding and loading was done by a Cat log loader, and a White Autocar logging truck with an attached jinker trailer hauled the logs to the mill.

I was also responsible for CNGT's production thinning operations. The hoop pine plantations were located between Bulolo township and the mature klinkii pine logging areas. This was because the plantations were planted by the Department of Forests in the first areas where the original klinkii pine forest had been logged. The hoop pine was still too small to be clear-felled, but the plantations did require thinning to release the best trees from competition so that the final crop could increase in girth more quickly. The thinning crew was trained to select the best trees to remain, and then the chainsaw operators felled the remainder. Our only native machine operator at that time, Leke Avora, extracted them using an old model Timberjack skidder.

Leke Avora was a bit of a rarity in New Guinea. He was born of a New Guinea native *meri* who had been raped by a Japanese soldier during the Second World War. The act of Japanese soldiers raping native women during the occupation of PNG during the war was extremely common. It happened everywhere that the Japs went, and on a significant scale. The birth of mixed Japanese-New Guinean babies was obviously an inevitable result. What wasn't common was the survival of these mixed-race babies.

The New Guinea natives hated the Japanese with a vengeance because of their brutality and savagery during the

59

occupation of PNG. Many New Guinea natives fought with the Allies and aided the Australian and New Zealand troops in any way possible to help defeat and inflict casualties upon the Japanese. The hatred was such that when a Japanese-fathered baby was born to any native *meri*, the baby was taken by the village *Sanguma*, its brains were dashed out on a rock, and the body was taken out into the bush.

Accordingly, any surviving product of a Japanese rape was extremely rare. It is said that the very few mixed babies that did survive to adulthood were the result of the mother going bush before the baby was born, staying well clear of her village, and attaching herself to a Mission Station where the baby would be raised with the help and protection of the Missionaries. Leke Avora was one such survivor and the only one that I personally knew in my five years in PNG.

Once extracted, the hoop pine thinnings were stacked along the roadside by the skidder ready for loading and transport to the sawmill. Although the thinnings were relatively small in diameter and the conversion rate was very poor, they were sawn up in the CNGT sawmill into small dimension construction timber for local use.

The truck that we used to haul the thinnings to the mill was a beat-up Albion with a fixed chassis and an old Hiab self-loading crane mounted on the back. The Albion had two high stanchions on each side to secure the logs, which were always piled up as high as possible. The full load was secured with a single chain load binder around the centre of the load. This was tightened with an over-centre binder lever.

Before I took over the thinning operations there had been quite a few worker accidents, so I spent a lot of time drumming safety practices into the workers and operators. One habit that they had was allowing the thinning crew workers, or even hitch-hiking local villagers, to ride on the top of the log loads as far as the mill. I hammered it into them that this was dangerous and that if the load ever moved, the chain broke, or the truck rolled, they would be history. I kept on and on about this, but the drivers kept letting their *wantoks* (mates) ride on the load when they thought that I wasn't looking. I eventually threatened that any of my crew caught riding on the load would be sacked on the spot. This seemed to work, and for a few weeks after that I didn't catch anyone riding on the logs.

Then, one afternoon, I was driving into town from the main logging camp to pick up some spare parts. I came around a corner, and here was the Albion lying on its side with a full load of thinnings spilled up the bank. The truck had swerved to avoid an oncoming local village taxi truck, the left side wheels had dropped into the drain, the truck had tipped onto its side, and the chain had broken, spilling the load. The driver was sitting on the roof of the truck with his head in his hands, although apparently uninjured.

I pulled to a stop and asked him what had happened. He was incoherent and babbling. I asked him if he was injured and what had happened, but he kept pointing to the pile of logs.

I said, "Yes, I can see those. We will have to get Leke with the skidder to pull them out, so we can get the truck back onto its wheels."

He continued muttering, "*Tupela boi i stap, masta. Tupela boi i stap.*"

Finally, I got the message. There were apparently two *bois* somewhere underneath the pile of logs. They had been riding on top of the load and, when the logs rolled off, they went with them. My heart dropped into my guts. I told the driver to stay where he was, turned around and raced back to the thinning operations to get Leke and his Timberjack. While I was driving, I radioed to Helen at the office and told her to phone the hospital and get the Doc out to the accident site, pronto!

Once I had got Leke on his way with the skidder, I grabbed two of the thinning crew, raced back to the Albion, and with the driver's help the four of us tried to manually roll the logs off the top of the heap and down onto the road. We couldn't make much headway, as the logs were crossed over and tangled.

As soon as Leke arrived on his machine, we started to drag the logs backwards off the truck, but it was slow going—too slow! Eventually we found the two *bois* in the middle of the load. They had been crushed to death. I was devastated. The Doc had arrived by this time but obviously couldn't do anything, so we loaded the *bois'* bodies into the back of my truck and took them away to the hospital.

I had seen a few dead bodies by now, but this time it was different. It was personal. These were my *bois*. In fact, they were two of my better plantation workers whom I had been training up, and their skill levels had been improving. I felt sick to my stomach and believed that I must somehow have been to blame for these deaths. My friends were very sympathetic and assured me that it wasn't my fault and that I had done everything that I could to prevent it, but that still didn't make it any easier to accept.

White Man's Magic

We had just finished midday *kai kai* (lunch) out in the logging camp one day and were having a brew. Andouri, one of my felling crew, came running into the camp shouting, *"Masta, masta, yupela kam kwiktaim! Kinoi na Arto i laik dai!"* ("Boss, boss, come quickly! Kinoi and Arto are very sick!").

Kinoi and Arto were our oldest and most senior and skilled crosscutters. They were the guys who felled the big trees on the logging operation. They were also Sepik elders, well respected within the company and the local Sepik workers' community. I grabbed a couple of the crew, and we followed Andouri into the forest where we found the two men under a big *Cryptocarya* tree. They were lying down and appeared to be in a kind of trance—pale, sweating, eyes wide and staring. Neither of them appeared able to speak. Yet there was no evidence of accident or injury to either of them.

We called up some more of the crew, and they carried the two men back to the logging camp and loaded them into the back of my ute. With four *bois* supporting them, I drove as fast as I dared into town and delivered them to the *haus sik* (hospital) in Bulolo. The Aussie doctor immediately carried out detailed examinations and tests on the pair but could not find any obvious reason for their illness and condition.

We left Kinoi and Arto at the hospital for the doctor to try to make a diagnosis and returned to the bush. When I arrived back in Bulolo that evening, I went straight around to the hospital to see how they were getting on. The doctor was still at a loss to find answers, and the men still couldn't (or wouldn't) speak or eat, although they had managed to drink a little water. The following evening they seemed weaker, and their wives and the other Sepiks were afraid that they were going to die.

I rounded up those of the felling crew who had been working nearby when the two men were taken ill, and we sat down together to discuss the problem. They were all close friends of the two sick men, as well as being workmates. After some rather protracted discussions, I eventually discovered that they believed the two men to be ill because they had been cursed with a magic spell that had been put on them by a *masalai* (a Kukukuku spirit that could take the shape of a man, or a dog, or whatever else took its fancy).

The klinkii pine logging area was located on the main divide between the Bulolo and Watut Valleys near the border of Kukukuku country. The Watuts, who are a major sub-tribe of the Kukukukus, believed that the *masalai* lived in the tops of the klinkii pines and the tall *Canarium* trees that grew among the klinkiis. The Watuts believed that when a klinkii pine was felled, the *masalai* living in that tree would leap onto the closest *Canarium* tree. If that *Canarium* tree was felled, however, the *masalai* would fly into a terrible rage and would be out for serious vengeance. Out of respect for the local cultural beliefs, we had long banned the felling of all *Canarium* trees.

The felling crew believed that Kinoi and Arto would almost certainly die; the two men themselves would believe this, too. The *bois* told me that the only possible way to cure Kinoi and Arto was to somehow find some stronger magic to drive out the curse that the *masalai* had put on them.

I took a couple of the *bois* back to the hospital with me and had a talk to the doctor. He gave Kinoi and Arto an injection of a mild stimulant, which seemed to pep them up a bit. The *bois* and I sat with the pair for a couple of hours, speaking in a mixture of Sepik and Pidgin, and persuaded them to tell us what had happened on the day they were taken ill. Eventually we managed to piece together the following story.

Kinoi and Arto had felled a big klinkii pine that morning. As it fell, the klinkii had smashed into a *Canarium* tree that was next to it and broken the top out of the *Canarium*. As there were broken branches and part of the main stem hanging down from the *Canarium*, the pair decided that in the interests of safety they should cut the remains of the tree down.

Soon afterwards, the two men sat down under a nearby *Cryptocarya* tree to eat their lunch. They had thrown some food scraps around the tree behind them, then dozed off to sleep. They awoke with a start to find themselves confronted by a filthy, evil-smelling little man with greasy, tangled hair that hung almost to the ground. They knew immediately that he was a *masalai* or Kukukuku evil spirit. They were naturally terrified. The little man was raging in anger and screamed at them that they had cut down the *Canarium* tree that he was living in.

Because Kinoi and Arto had decided to fell the damaged *Canarium* tree, it seemed that the *masalai* had been forced to jump into the adjacent *Cryptocarya* tree that the men sat under to have their lunch. To add insult to injury, the men had thrown their food waste under this tree, and this had incensed the *masalai* even further. The *masalai* had pointed his skinny finger at Kinoi and Arto and told them he was putting a curse on them — they would get very sick, become unable to walk or eat, and they would die. Upon uttering his curse, the *masalai* had vanished into the forest. The two Sepiks had then attempted to stand up but found themselves unable to do so, and they had collapsed in a state of shock. They were both totally convinced that they were going to die and that there was nothing anyone could do about it.

Once we had established the reason behind their sickness, I sat down with the Aussie doctor to discuss the situation. Eventually we came up with a cunning plan. I went back to Kinoi and Arto and explained to them that we now understood the problem, and we believed their story that their illness was the result of a curse that had been put on them by the Kukukuku *masalai*. I then explained to them that the doctor had managed to obtain some even stronger magic than the *masalai* had used and that he would be able to remove the curse. He would achieve this by making Kinoi and Arto unconscious, after which he would cut them open and remove the evil spirits from inside their bodies. He would then send the spirits down to Lae where they would be thrown into the sea, where of course they would die. As everyone knows, sea water is deadly poisonous to *masalai* evil spirits! The doctor would then bring the two men back to consciousness, and the evil spirits would be gone.

Convincing the two men that this was all going to work took another day and a lot of persuasion, but eventually they agreed to give it a try, as they believed this was their only hope of survival. Kinoi and Arto were wheeled off to the operating room with due ceremony, put under anaesthetic, and then later brought round again.

Once they awoke, the doctor assured Kinoi and Arto that the evil spirits had been duly removed and had died

66

when they were thrown into the sea at Lae. The following morning after a good night's sleep, they both agreed that they felt almost completely recovered and were ready to return to work. They thanked the doctor for his powerful medicine, walked out of the hospital, climbed into the back of my ute, rolled a *puse*, and we all headed back to the logging camp. Upon arrival, they put away a meal produced by the *cook-bois* and spent the morning resting before going back to work in the jungle as if nothing had happened.

Sorcery, spirits, magic, *sanguma, pouri pouri* (call it what you will) is a huge presence and reality in the lives of almost all New Guineans. Its influence is not always malign though; the *Sanguma* (witchdoctor) is both feared and respected in the villages. He is seen as a keeper of the culture, a kind of high priest to the spirits of the wind, the water, and the trees.

The constant menace of sorcery is a daily presence in PNG though. A man must make sure that no part of his body wastes—his nail parings, hair, or excreta—should never come into the possession of a rival, because these can be used to work a spell against the owner. Among many tribes, the belief still persists that all deaths are due to magic, and sometimes old women, specifically, are "smelled out" and killed as witches if someone in the tribe dies.

Consequently, everyone treated the event with the *Canarium* tree very seriously as though it was the most natural thing in the world, and life carried on as usual. That was, however, the last *Canarium* tree that was ever felled out in the Watut, that is for sure.

The Dreaded Death Adder

One of the nastiest pieces of work that ever slithered in the Bulolo, Wau, and Watut Valleys was the death adder. These little beasts are very common throughout PNG but appeared to be extremely prevalent in the bush and—more especially—the *kunai* grass-covered hills south of the Watut River. The death adder is a brownish-grey colour that blends in perfectly with the undergrowth and *kunai* grass, making them very difficult to see. If trodden on or even lightly touched, they will immediately strike. Fatalities from death adder bites are very much a reality and very common in much of rural PNG.

Death adders *(Acanthophis* species*)* are nocturnal as well as diurnal, which makes them doubly dangerous, as they can be active at any time. They are about two to three feet long with a triangular shaped head, a short thick body, and a short, pencil-shaped tail. They will raise and wriggle their short, worm-like tails to lure prey such as lizards, birds, and small mammals to within striking distance. They have a bad habit of sitting under cover during the day, often close to pathways along which small animals (and humans) regularly travel.

Death adder venom is highly potent and contains toxins that cause paralysis, muscle failure, and suffocation due to paralysis of the throat muscles. The venom is absorbed into the bloodstream in less than 15 minutes. An untreated death adder bite can cause death within two to six hours depending on where on the body and how close to an artery the venom was injected. Generally, to survive a death adder bite in a critical part of the body, an anti-venom injection needs to be given within one hour of the bite or within two hours if the bite is more superficial and lower down on the body. Failure to receive an anti-venom shot within that period can result in the person going into convulsions and the throat closing, causing suffocation and death.

In the area near Bulolo, the majority of Watut people bitten by death adders were *meris*. The *meris* walked for miles from their villages and gardens along narrow tracks through the bush and *kunai* grass to the mission station or the road-head. Their *bilums* would be full of *kaukau* and other vegetables to sell at the mission or the markets.

One morning, my road survey crew and I were working near a native walking track while locating a road line. At that time, I had only been working out in the bush a couple of months. A young Watut boy came running along the track. He was panting.

"Masta, masta, wanpela meri i laik dai! Sinek i kaikai em long hap long Watut!" He was telling me: "Boss, boss, there is a *meri* who is very sick! She has been bitten by a snake over in the Watut!"

Within about 20 minutes, two Watut men arrived carrying a little old *meri* between them. The *meri* didn't look too good, and I asked them how long ago she had been bitten.

Watuts (like all New Guinea natives) have only a vague sense of time and distance (at least when trying to convey such information to a third party), so I knew that if we could get the time fixed to within half a day we would be doing well. They assured me, however, that she was bitten *"monen taim long maunten kunai"* ("morning time in the *kunai* grass hills"). This made sense, as she would likely have been walking down the *kunai* grass hills from her village to the road-head, her *bilum* bag loaded with *kaukau*, somewhere between seven and eight in the morning. It was now ten o'clock.

I could see that she was in a bad way, so I got my road crew to take over carrying duties from the two Watuts who were looking pretty exhausted, and we all jogged as fast as we could along the track to where I had left the Jeep. We lay the *meri* down in the back with the three Watuts supporting her and one of my men in the passenger's seat, and I took off, driving as fast as I could, heading for Bulolo and the hospital. The tracks near our work area were very rough, so the badly sprung jeep was bouncing around all over the place, and the men in the back were hanging onto the old girl for dear life. It was about forty minutes to the hospital at the speed I was going, and about half-way there the *meri* started to go into convulsions. I slammed on the brakes, grabbed a stick off the side of the road and jammed it sideways into her mouth to prevent her from biting her tongue off, and then I instructed the *bois* how to hold her so that she didn't injure herself. She was thrashing around a bit though and was showing surprising strength for a skinny little *meri*. We ended up with a *boi* holding onto one arm each and the third sitting on her to keep her immobilised.

We finally made the hospital and roused the doctor, who immediately gave her an anti-venom shot, followed by another injection to help to relieve the oncoming throat paralysis—all while she was still lying in the back of my grotty, dust covered jeep. In this case, speed was more important than hygiene!

Shortly afterward, the *bois* carried the *meri* into the hospital, and I left her in the care of the boy and two men who had accompanied her. I collected my own man from the hospital, and we headed back out to the bush.

That evening, I drove up to the hospital, found a nurse I knew and asked her how the old *meri* was that we had brought in that morning. I didn't think she had had much more than a 50:50 chance, especially as she had already started convulsing before we got to the hospital. The nurse told me that she was, amazingly, still alive! The medical staff hadn't thought she had much of a chance when we brought her in, either. They figured that she was over the worst of it now though, as the Doc had fed a catheter down her throat before she went into paralysis and her throat closed. She had survived through the convulsion phase and was still breathing, so the nurse assured me that she would most likely recover.

That first outcome was a good one, but over the next three years I brought in from the bush to the hospital around a dozen Watuts who had been bitten by death adders. Of those, three died because they were already too far gone by the time their rescuers reached me. One *meri* died on the way to hospital in the back of my ute, even though I drove like a lunatic all the way. She had been bitten quite a few hours before the villagers got her to where I was working.

The risk of being bitten by death adders was the reason for a practice followed by many bushmen (myself included) in PNG when walking along bush, scrub, or *kunai* grass tracks. This was known as "the third man", and it had nothing to do with Orson Welles. Because of the narrow bush tracks, it was only possible to walk in single file. The Boss always walked third in line. The first and second men in line were usually local villagers or the Boss's crew. The system worked thus: Although he didn't know it, the first man's role was to wake up any death adders that might be sleeping near the track. The second man's job was to get bitten if the snake missed the first man. The boss, of course, walked third and, therefore, had a significantly reduced chance of being bitten.

At least that was the theory, and of course numbers one and two were never made aware of their critical position in the scheme of things! In all the years that I trekked through the jungles of PNG and Irian Jaya (Indonesian West Papua) as third man, I never got bitten by a death adder. I guess that proves the value of the third man theory. Mind you, none of the first or second men in my party ever got bitten either. I never came really close to being bitten by a death adder until ten years later when I was working in Irian Jaya, but that's another story for another book.

A Fine, Upstanding Citizen

In 1968, the PNG Police decided that they needed an independent volunteer constabulary located in all the main outback locations to be made up solely of resident expatriates. The idea was that, in the event of a riot or major inter-tribal conflict anywhere around the country, particularly in areas where some of the participants of the riot or tribal conflict were from the same tribe as the local police force, there would be a trained, independent force that could be trucked or flown in to help sort things out.

The problem in PNG was the system of *wantok* (which means "originating from the same tribe or village"), and this played out with the native police never acting against, arresting, or clobbering members of their own tribe, even if they were the instigators of a riot or had committed murder and mayhem. So, the police held a recruitment drive by approaching individual expats whom they considered to be physically fit, fine, law-abiding, upstanding citizens and convincing them to join up for training and eventual qualification as reserve constables in the Royal Papua New Guinea Reserve Constabulary.

Jim Riley and I were two of ten expats approached in Bulolo and who agreed to join up. It was all good fun, in actual fact. We attended a two-hour training session three nights a week and received instruction in the Queensland criminal code, riot control, use of clubs, and martial arts, got tear gassed in an enclosed space, and were generally trained up to become "The Fuzz". The main instructor was the local Police Chief Inspector, but outside trainers were brought in from Lae and even Brisbane for some specialised subjects. Training lasted the best part of a year, and after passing our final exams we graduated as reserve constables. Unfortunately, we never did get to attend a riot or bash any heads before I left Bulolo, which was a bit of a disappointment after all that effort and training.

The one downside of being a cop was that you were expected to attend post mortems if you were available. All corpses in PNG, regardless of how or when the person died, had to have a post mortem conducted. The local doctor carried out the post mortems, but each one had to be attended by a member of the police. Even before we had graduated, we reserve constables were expected to front up to post mortems if a regular force policeman was unavailable. The local policemen, all Tolais from the Rabaul area of New Britain Island, usually managed to avoid attending post mortems because they were out on patrol, or they had a head-ache, or some other excuse.

Regretably, that meant that we were frequently called upon for this unpleasant task. Generally, the doctor would round up whoever happened to be closest and available at the time. Most of us reserve constables, including those from CNGT and the Department of Forests, spent our working days out in the jungle, although there were a couple of reserve constables who worked at the ply mill. Most of us were, as a consequence, unable to be contacted during the day. This meant that someone had to be sent to find one of the reservists and get him back to town.

A real disadvantage of the company fitting a radio telephone into my ute was that I became easier to contact than anyone else. Hence, I tended to get roped into attending post mortems more often than most of the others. I found a way to sidestep many of the post mortems, however, when the CNGT office radio shack and telephone exchange was taken over by the lovely Helen. Helen had recently returned home from boarding school in Australia, and she quickly nominated herself as a very, very close personal friend of mine and would do practically anything if she thought it was in my best interests. When she received a call from the hospital looking for me, Helen would tell them that she couldn't contact me or that I was out in the bush and had gone walkabout for the day, or any other excuse that she could think up on the spur of the moment. She would then try to contact one of the other reservists and rope them into doing the job instead.

The post mortems were carried out in the hospital morgue, which was a tin shed down in a gulley under some trees about 100 metres from the main hospital buildings. The official police post mortem duties were to observe and witness the work of the doctor, apparently for legal reasons. All the post mortems I attended were those of natives. I didn't mind the fresh ones so much, although I preferred to observe the procedure from outside the door looking in. The smells weren't quite so bad out there in the fresh air.

There were, however, a couple of post mortems that I got trapped into attending when Helen was either unable or not quick enough to engineer my escape. These were both Watut natives. One had been bitten and killed by a death adder, and the other had an arrow through him. Neither of these guys had been reported missing or their bodies found for over two weeks after they had died. Any dead body, human or otherwise, that has lain out in the scrub or the *kunai* grass in the PNG heat and humidity for two weeks is going to be grossly offensive to the olfactory senses by the time it is recovered. Even though the Doc gave me a surgical mask to wear, it did little to muffle the putrid stench. I got around the second one (which was very bad) by borrowing a pair of binoculars off a mate and sitting up on the hill about fifty metres from the morgue, observing proceedings through the binoculars. I'm not sure if that was permitted under the Queensland Criminal Code on post mortems, regulation such and such, section blankety-blank, but the Doc promised that he wouldn't tell anyone if I didn't.

Jim and I were keen on guns, being Kiwi Forest Rangers. Possession of any firearm other than a shotgun was illegal in PNG at that time, unless you were a police officer or member of the military—although there was some illegal stuff around. Some guy in Lae gave Jim an old .45 revolver. It was an ancient six-shooter like the cowboys used in the Wild West. Unfortunately, it only came with a handful of .45 cartridges, and we were unable to source any more. After a bit of searching around, Jim discovered that Jimmy Seeto down in Lae carried stocks of various calibre cartridges, which he kept secured out the back. Jimmy Seeto's was one of those Chinese shops you find in out-of-the-way places that sell and deal in almost everything.

Jimmy Seeto couldn't get any .45 calibre rimmed revolver cartridges either, but he did have .44 calibre cartridges with recessed rims designed to be used in automatic weapons. The .44 size bullets could be used in a .45 calibre barrel and revolving chamber, but of course the recessed rim meant that they dropped straight through the chamber. Jim and I fixed that problem by sitting down at his *donga* one Saturday afternoon with a couple of SPs and some side-cutters. We crimped out the recessed rims of the .44s with the side-cutters to make flanges so that the cartridges would hold up in the .45 revolver chamber. Probably not the safest thing to do in hindsight, but we managed to doctor up a hundred rounds or so without blowing our fingers off.

We would take the old revolver out into the bush and bang away at targets nailed to a tree. The old six-gun had a kick like a mule, but even at fifteen metres the thing was hopelessly inaccurate. The barrel was badly worn, and of course the .44 calibre cartridges were fractionally smaller in diameter than the .45 barrel, so the bullet would roll coming out of the muzzle and hit the target sideways. The only thing we ever actually shot with that revolver was a *bilak bokis* (flying fox) hanging in a tree. We were on a small island off Kui on the north coast at the time, and—to be fair—there were hundreds of *bilak bokis* hanging upside down in one huge mass in a dead tree. They were so close together that there was a 99 percent chance of hitting at least one, even if you closed your eyes and just pointed in the general direction.

One day, Jim and I were up at the Bulolo Police Station after a reserve constabulary training session, and Dave, the cop, showed us his collection of confiscated hand guns that he kept in his safe. All these guns had been confiscated from expatriates over a number of years or handed in when they left PNG. The only way that a native could have got hold of one was to steal it, and that rarely happened. Among his collection, Dave had a nice .32 Beretta automatic pistol, which looked like a real mafia-type hand gun, and a Bernardelli .22 automatic.

Jim and I were handling and admiring these pieces enviously, so big-hearted Dave, who was always on the lookout to make a quick buck, sold them to us for a nominal sum. I took the Beretta .32, which looked like it had seen very little use and had a bore that was practically pristine, and Jim took the Bernardelli. We were able to buy ammo for both of these guns at Jimmy Seetos. Many happy hours were spent out in the bush blasting away at targets. Because they had seen very little use, both guns were very accurate at short distances. Considerable practice was required to master accurate shooting with a hand gun though, especially as we had been shooting all our lives with long rifles.

Our gallant leader of the Royal PNG Reserve Constabulary, benefactor in the matter of illegal firearms, and general upholder of the law, Police Inspector Dave, was a bit of a maverick. He had been known to over-indulge in the old SP Lager on more than one occasion. That couldn't be held against him in a place like Bulolo until the day that he was presented with a brand new Land Rover fire engine. It was a handsome machine and much admired by all—at least during the three days that he had it! Big Dave had been drinking up at the Pine Lodge Hotel this particular night until he was practically legless. Then somewhere about midnight, Dave decided to take his brand-new fire engine for a test drive.

The next morning, our gallant Police Chief turned up at the CNGT workshop to ask if he could borrow the company tow truck to help him out of a bit of bother up the Bulolo Valley road towards Wau. One of the workshop mechanics drove the tow truck out to the site and discovered the Bulolo Police Force's brand-new Land Rover fire engine over a bank at the bottom of a steep gulley and lying on its side in a creek—clearly a write-off! The wreck was trucked down to Lae and never seen again. Our Dave had the riot act read to him over that little lot!

The *Tangimoana*

One of the Aussie dozer operators working on the road construction was a bloke called Chook Lear. Chook was 32 years old and somewhat overweight, as he spent all day sitting on his tractor. He was a big eater and socked back more than a few stubbies of SP every night after work at the Bowling Club. Chook had married a very nice Aussie girl and, after about six years of trying, his wife had finally become pregnant with their first child.

There had been a few thefts, mainly of clothing, from the *woss-woss* (the laundry, usually located some 15-20 metres from each house) of some of the married quarters on the street closest to one of the native compounds. Chook's *woss-woss* had been raided a couple of times previously, and on this particular night he was looking outside when he spotted a native climbing out of the window of the *woss-woss* with an armful of clothes. Chook had just finished dinner and was dressed only in his *lap-lap*. He shouted at the miscreant, dived out the back door, and gave chase. The robber dropped the clothes and took off like a rat up a drainpipe, sprinting along the grass verge in the direction of the native quarters.

Chook was determined that he was not going to let the thief get away this time, so at about the 50-metre mark he put on a burst of speed to try to catch up with the culprit. Unfortunately, Chook's years of physical inactivity, heavy eating and drinking—coupled with an impressive waistline, and an obviously dicky ticker—finally caught up with him, and he fell flat on his face on the grass. The Doc said he had suffered a massive heart attack and was dead before he hit the ground. A very sad event indeed, and there was universal sympathy for his young wife and unborn baby.

Mrs Chook sold all the big stuff, then packed up the rest and returned to Australia to live with her parents. Chook had been a good builder and handyman, and he and a mate from Lae had been building a boat in a shed up near the Forestry compound. The boat had been finished (except for some painting) only a few weeks before Chook died. It was a 21 foot Hartley cabin cruiser, a good sized, roomy boat that was built to a tried and tested design. Chook had also had a solid boat trailer built, and the boat was completed while sitting in the shed on the trailer. Chook had paid for the boat and trailer construction, and his mate was going to supply the engine. In fact, his mate had bought a 165 hp Mercruiser inboard-outboard with a stern leg, which was still in its box down in Lae.

Jim and I decided that this was a good opportunity to acquire ourselves a boat and explore the north coast of New Guinea from sea level. We made Chook's widow a fair offer for the boat and trailer, which she accepted. Then we duly completed the painting and named our new boat *Tangimoana* (Maori for "lament of the ocean").

We started negotiations with Chook's mate in Lae to buy the Mercruiser, but we felt that he was being a bit greedy and wanted too much for it. In the end we bought a new 120 hp Volvo Penta inboard-outboard petrol engine with stern leg from the Volvo-Penta dealer in Lae, and we installed it ourselves.

We towed the *Tangimoana* down to Lae and launched her at South Pacific Timber's log barge unloading beach at

Voco Point. We stored the boat in Lae at a mate's place, as it was too far—and the road was too bad—to easily tow it back to Bulolo. Jim and I would drive the 106 kilometres to Lae about every second weekend or so, depending on the weather, launch the *Tangimoana*, and head south-east along the coast to Kui, Buso, and the Longuerue Islands.

There are dozens of beautiful islands and atolls in the Longuerue group, all uninhabited except for the biggest island, Lasanga. These islands are only a few kilometres off the coast, all surrounded by untouched coral reefs.

The reefs were alive with fish, clams, crayfish, and the most amazing coloured coral we had ever seen. We would fish, snorkel, spearfish, catch crayfish, and sleep on the white sandy beaches on the islands. Sometimes we would take a couple of the girls from Bulolo up to the islands for the weekend—there was never any shortage of volunteers to crew on the *Tangimoana*!

There was a mainland village called Buso on the beach just north of Kui Bay, which was not far from the Longuerue group of islands. Buso was on the opposite side of the Kui river mouth to the Department of Forests camp. We knew one of the forestry guys from the camp—his name was Gobu, and he came from Buso village. Through Gobu we became friends with the villagers at Buso, and we would usually drop them off some fish when we caught more than we needed.

Sometimes, we towed Titi, Buso's village chief, out to the Islands in his outrigger canoe. We would anchor in a lagoon inside one of the atolls and wait until the sun went down. Once it got dark, Jim and I would get into the canoe with Titi. One of us would paddle, another would direct the beam of the kerosene pressure lamp hanging off a forked stick in the prow and watch for fish and turtles, while the third person would balance with one foot on either side of the canoe, holding one of Titi's fishing spears. One spear was multi-pronged, and this was used to spear the long thin garfish (similar to New Zealand piper, only bigger and with teeth), which swam on the surface. The second spear was a three-pronged job for spearing larger fish, which swam at half a metre or so deep, and the third was a heavy, single-pronged spear for spearing turtles.

There were many turtles around the reefs, and they were a favourite food of the coastal villagers. Jim, Titi, and I took turns at spearing the fish, but we generally left the turtle spearing to Titi. We would locate a turtle within spearing depth, Titi would spear it, and I would dive into the water on top of it. Grabbing the turtle by the edge of its shell, I would pull it off the spear, turn it upside down, and flip it into the canoe. I got pretty good at that.

After we caught enough fish and two or three turtles, it was time to paddle over to a sandy beach near the anchored *Tangimoana*, collect some dead coconut fronds and firewood, and get a fire going. Eaten straight out of the embers, the grilled garfish were delicious!

At night we slept on the beach until the sun came up, then tied the canoe behind the Tangimoana and towed it back to Titi's village on the mainland. The whole village would turn out to meet us, and the fish and turtles were shared out among whole population. There was always great excitement on these occasions, and Jim and I enjoyed being considered part of the tribe.

Jim and I, being keen fisherman, enjoyed fishing around the islands. One of our favourite islands was Juani. It had good reefs, plenty of fish, and a good beach to sleep on. Another good island was Sayos, with its beautiful white coral atolls and beaches. The fishing was good, but we needed fresh bait each time we went out.

The first couple of times that we went down to the islands we didn't bring any bait, so we dived out on a reef and speared some garfish and other small reef fish to use. Whenever we went fishing after that, however, we went fully loaded. Before we left Bulolo, I raided my dynamite store and liberated half a dozen sticks of Semigel, a handful of detonators, and a coil of safety fuse to take with us.

On arrival down at the islands, we hunted around for a good school of oily bait fish such as mackerel, which often schooled over a shallow, sloping, sandy bottom just off a beach. I cut a stick of Semigel in half, crimped a short length of safety fuse into the detonator, and pushed it into the end of the half plug. I waited until a school of fish swam into the shallow water about 15 metres from the boat, lit the fuse, held it for about two seconds, and hurled it out into the middle of the school. The gelignite usually blew at about two metres causing only a small eruption on the surface when it exploded. Most of the school scattered when I threw the dynamite amongst them, but some were still close enough to be stunned by the shock wave. Some floated to the surface, some were suspended in mid-water, and a few sank to the sandy bottom.

We had bought a couple of multi-pronged spears from the villagers at Buso, and wearing our flippers and goggles, we dived over the side with these in hand. We swam around spearing the stunned and dead fish, flicking them into the boat as fast as we could. The reason for speed was that within about five minutes after the explosion, sharks began to arrive, homing in from all directions.

We had learned that explosions under-water automatically attracted sharks for miles around, as they somehow associated the sound, or the shock-wave, with food. The first group of sharks to appear tended to be smaller reef sharks that were probably already in the neighbourhood, and they weren't any threat to us, but very soon the big boys started cruising in. As soon as we spotted these big guys arriving, we took to our scrapers and practically swam straight up the side of the boat. There's nothing like suddenly having to share your swimming pool with a lot of teeth to get the adrenaline moving!

Jim and I were keen snorkel divers, and we spent a lot of time looking for new reefs and just snorkelling around looking at the myriad brilliantly coloured reef fish. The islands off Kui had some of the most pristine and original coral reefs left on earth at that time. There were miles of various coloured corals, and the fish life was incredible.

We always carried spear guns, which we used—when necessary—to dissuade nosy sharks that insisted on swimming up over the edge of a reef to see what we were all about. There were always plenty of reef sharks of all sizes around when we were diving, and they were very inquisitive. We didn't shoot at them, but if they came too close we would poke a spear at them, and they would veer off and do another circuit or two before heading off to wherever it was that they were going in the first place.

The beasties that we were more nervous of were the gangs of barracuda, which always swam together in small schools of about a dozen fish. They were not only inquisitive, but (unlike sharks) these guys worked together as a single unit. They swam with their mouths open, showing rows of long razor-sharp teeth, and were always aggressive and quite unafraid of us. They would cruise up over the edge of a reef and charge straight at us. They were a bit scary until we had developed some experience in how to deal with them. We soon learned that they reacted the same way as sharks if you turned to face them, stood upright in the water showing them as large a frontal surface as possible, and shouted and screamed as hard and as loudly as you could under-water. This confused and panicked them, and they would usually veer away and swim off. We didn't like to stay in the water too long though if the barracuda hung around, because we had been told by the local natives that you could never trust these buggers. They are just plain nasty.

The other denizens of the reef that we tended to keep an eye out for were the many species of sea snakes that lived around the shallow reefs. They were generally quite lazy swimmers and were not scared of us at all. Often, if we were spear-fishing or crayfishing, we would pull our head out from under a coral ledge to find ourselves face to face with a black and white, or red and white banded sea snake.

They weren't aggressive (fortunately) but just seemed to ignore everything in their path and would swim into you if you didn't move out of their way. Usually we would just gently tap them with the side of the spear and steer them off in another direction when they came too close. They were all deadly poisonous, and the venom from a bite from one of these little guys was enough to kill ten men in just a few minutes. Fortunately, however, they had very small mouths, and it was difficult for them to bite something as large around as a human limb. It was rare for someone to get bitten by these little critters, but nevertheless we treated them with the respect that they deserved.

One long weekend, Jim, myself, Herman the German (who was working on a project at the Forestry Department in Bulolo), and a couple of female Aussie school teachers from Lae headed down the coast to the Struggling Islands, which are a group of uninhabited islands some way south of the Longuerue Islands. We speared some fish, cooked them up on a beach on one of the islands, swam, snorkelled, and slept on the sand under the coconut palms. On the Sunday morning, Jim and I were snorkelling on a reef just off the island where we had camped, while Herman and the girls were splashing about and swimming in the crystal-clear water off the beach.

Herman was just walking out of the water when he let out a scream, which we heard over 100 metres away out on the reef. Jim and I swam as fast as we could back to the beach to find Herman lying on the beach, groaning in pain. The girls were trying to comfort him but had no idea what the problem was. Jim and I threw off our flippers and ran up the beach to where Herman was holding his foot with blood pouring out from under the sole. He was obviously in agony. After we calmed him down a bit, he told us that he had trodden on a fish buried in the sand—he only saw a flash of it as it swam away. A spine had driven into his foot as the fish wriggled away. The pain was excruciating, and the puncture wound was bleeding profusely. Jim and I looked at each other and said simultaneously, "Oh shit! A stonefish!"

This was something that we had always been afraid of around the islands, as these creatures were highly poisonous, and often deadly to humans depending on how many spines punctured the skin. Stonefish were common along the coast and around the islands we frequented, and it was a long way to anywhere to get the treatment and anti-venom necessary to counteract the poison. We knew that time was critical here. It all depended upon how much poison he had received but, without an anti-venom injection, Herman could very possibly die.

We quickly calculated that the two nearest towns that should have stonefish anti-venom available were Lae and Morobe. There were other villages on the mainland that were closer, but we doubted that any of those would have the anti-venom, as it had to be stored under refrigeration and these villages simply wouldn't have the facilities. We were closer to Morobe than we were to Lae, so we bandaged up Herman's foot with supplies from our first aid kit, helped him into the boat, and lay him flat on the floor with his foot raised. We swiftly loaded our gear into the boat and took off at full speed for Morobe.

The girls sat either side of Herman to hold him steady, as Jim had the throttle wide open and the boat was bouncing a bit in the light chop as we raced for the coast. We had never been to Morobe town before, so we hoped that it was equipped with a decent first aid station and perhaps even a *lik-lik* doctor. It took us an hour at full noise to get across to Morobe, and we pulled into what appeared to be the main jetty up a sheltered creek beside the town. There was nobody about, so Jim and I split up and trotted off in different directions to see if we could find someone who could tell us where the *haus sik* was located.

I eventually found a local man having a smoke under a coconut palm. He pointed back the way I had come and told me that the first aid post was on the small hill just above our landing stage, but nobody would be there because it was Sunday. He knew where the *lik-lik* doctor's house was though, and he said that if we could get the patient up to the *haus sik*, he would go and find the doctor and ask him to meet us there. He trotted off down the narrow dirt track (which I assumed was the main street), and I headed back, located Jim, and together we dragged Herman up the hill to the *haus sik* and deposited him on the verandah.

We had been there about 10 minutes when the *lik-lik* doctor came striding up and—once apprised of the situation—opened the clinic, retrieved his injection equipment from his bag and the stonefish anti-venom from out of the fridge, and gave Herman his shot while he was still lying there on the verandah. The Doc reckoned that was as good a place as any to treat a patient, and anyway, it was better that Herman didn't move around too much while the poison was still in his foot and leg. The *lik-lik* doctor also gave Herman another injection to dull the pain. He then removed a small piece of broken spine from the wound in Herman's foot, packed the wound with antibiotic powder, and bandaged it up.

Once all this was over, the Doc said that we would be wise to stay where we were for at least a couple of hours so that he could keep an eye on the patient and check his reaction to the anti-venom. He said that if Herman got worse, he might have to give him another shot. He reckoned that Herman appeared to have been rather lucky, as only one spine seemed to have pierced his foot, and this would have limited the amount of venom that he received.

The *lik-lik* doctor went off home to finish his breakfast while we collected some tucker from the boat and made ourselves some sandwiches on the clinic verandah. Herman wasn't interested in food; the pain in his foot soon eased, and he dozed off to sleep. After an hour or so, the *lik-lik* doctor returned, checked Herman out, and declared him fit enough to travel back to Lae.

We took our time cruising back to Lae while trying to keep the motion of the boat as smooth as possible for Herman's comfort. He was feeling a lot better when we arrived in Lae, so we drove straight back to Bulolo and got the Bulolo doctor to check him out. Fortunately, we had done all the right things, and Herman recovered fully within a few days, although he was limping around for a while.

Crocodile Hunting

In 1968, I spent some time with our sister company, South Pacific Timbers, looking at some new hardwood forest resources near Lae and reviewing the logging operations at Kui down the coast. I took one of the local Forestry Rangers with me, and we initially spent a few days cutting tracks and surveying through some dense jungle about an hour north of Lae. We camped out in the bush, as there were no villages in the area, but we found some good forest with some good-sized commercial *Anispotera* and *Pometia pinnata* (taun) species. We also found a number of beautiful streams and waterfalls deep in the jungle. We set up our camp near one of them so we had somewhere to clean up and source our drinking water.

Following the Lae stint, I caught a ride to Kui on the company log barge, *Baiune,* which had just unloaded logs from Kui at Voco Point in Lae. The return trip to Kui Bay was about five hours, as we only carried a light load of food supplies and spare parts for the logging camp. I stayed at the Kui Logging camp for a few weeks and reviewed the logging and barge loading operations. It was only a small camp staffed by two Australians, about twenty native loggers, and the Bush Boss, Lloyd Mitchum. There was also a native cook who could come up with a pretty good feed, and then there was the German mechanic, Klaus, who regarded himself as an expert in making sauerkraut.

Klaus would process all the cabbage he could lay his hands on, and when he thought it was rotten enough, he would stash it in the freezer. The freezer was an electric job, powered by electricity from a gen-set located up behind the workshop. The generator had broken down a week before I arrived, and the barge I was travelling on carried a replacement. Nobody opened the freezer for a few days; they thought it might keep the food cooler if they kept the lid closed. When they finally got around to opening it, not only had the meat inside it gone rotten, but Klaus's sauerkraut had literally grown legs and was trying to escape from the freezer and take over the world. Talk about putrid! You could smell the stench down at the dock when we arrived. Even after they had buried the stuff, the stink hung around the camp for weeks!

One Saturday night some of the Sepik loggers asked me if I would like to go hunting *pukpuks* (crocodiles) with them. I said I was keen, and so the *bois* turned up at about 10 p.m. with a couple of spotlights, a shotgun, and a pocketful of rifled 12 bore slugs. A rifled slug is a single projectile packed into a 12-gauge shotgun cartridge with rifling around the projectile to make it spin inside the smooth barrel of the shotgun. This vastly improves the accuracy. The bore size of a 12-gauge is 0.729", but the calibre of a solid slug is smaller at 0.690" so it can clear the choke. They also had a mongrel dog in tow, which they had "borrowed" from the local village.

We walked up a track behind the camp that ran alongside the Paiawa River for about 1.5 kilometres until we came to a branch where a creek ran into the river. This was where the *bois* had found some fresh *pukpuk* tracks a few days before. They tied the dog up at the edge of the creek, collected a handful of stones, and we all climbed up some nearby trees overlooking the dog and the creek.

The dog was apparently the bait. *Pukpuks* are very fond of dog and can smell one from some considerable distance away. Shortly after dark, the *bois* started throwing stones at the dog to make it bark in order to make it easier for the *pukpuk* to find.

We had been up in the trees for nearly an hour when we heard a sloshing noise coming down the creek. The dog started going berserk and trying to climb the tree that it was tied to. We waited silently until we could clearly hear the *pukpuk* coming nearer to the dog. Then I switched on the spotlight that I was holding, and there at the foot of a tree was a three metre salt-water crocodile, just in the process of winding up for a lunge at the dog. The red eyes reflected in the spotlight, and the guy with the shotgun lined him up: Boom! There was much thrashing about in the creek with water spraying everywhere. The dog almost died of apoplexy and strangulation on its tether.

After a short while, when we figured that it was safe enough, we clambered down from our trees to suss the damage. Our hunter was a good shot and had hit the *pukpuk* right between the eyes. The 12-gauge rifled slug was lethal at such a close range. Result: one dead *pukpuk*. We cut some poles and rattan vines, trussed the croc up, and carried him home.

Next morning, the *bois* skinned the *pukpuk* and divided up the meat between our worker's camp, the loggers' camp, and the local village that lent us the bait-dog. Fresh *pukpuk* is excellent meat with very good flavour and texture. The *bois* stretched the skin and dried it to sell to Jimmy Seeto on their next trip to Lae.

Adventure on the Open Sea

One long weekend, Jim and I decided that we should take the *Tangimoana* and explore the remote and mysterious Tami Islands.

The Tami Islands are a small group of islands located some 95 kilometres east of the port of Lae in the Huon Gulf. The Islanders are known for their distinctive wooden bowls, religious figure carvings and ceremonial masks. The largest island is not more than about 80 metres across.

Jim and I loaded up fuel, food, and a carton of SP, and launched the *Tangimoana* at Voco Point in Lae early on a Saturday morning. With chart in hand, we headed off on a compass bearing for the Tami Islands. The weather was good, the sea was flat with just a slight swell, and we were having a good run. We steered due east for the first 50 kilometres or so, keeping about five kilometres off the mainland coast to avoid reefs until we were abeam of Bua village near the tip of Cape Gernards.

At that point we changed our heading to east-northeast on a direct course to the Tami Islands. The Tami Islands are very low atolls, no more than about 1.8 metres above sea level (plus the height of the coconut palms), so we needed to be accurate with our navigation as we wouldn't sight the islands until we were almost upon them. We were well out from land and heading for open sea with no land in sight ahead of us, which was a bit of a concern. My main worry was that the Volvo Penta could break down on us out there. We had no alternative means of propulsion, no radio, and no flares—not that the latter would have been of any use, as there was no coastguard or any powered vessels in the area to react to them.

We were cruising at around eighteen knots, so the trip from Lae, with a calm sea and light breeze, should have taken us about three hours provided we didn't veer too far off course. We had been running for about two hours and were well out in the open ocean when we spotted a speck on the horizon almost directly ahead of us. We quickly came upon it, sighting our first ever Tami Island canoe. Both Jim and I found it fascinating!

It was about thirty feet long with a single outrigger and two large, square coconut matting sails, and it was sailing on the same heading that we were. Although it had a single outrigger like most of the other coastal craft, Tami Island canoes are totally unique in design and decoration. They are large, ocean-going canoes about thirty feet long with curved ends and carved prows and they are hewn from a single straight log. The sides are built up with wide, hand–hewn boards. Each board is at least fifty centimetres wide and runs the entire length of the canoe in a single piece. These sides are painted in designs of red and white, the whole canoe is bound together with plant fibre, and the joints are caulked with tree gum. The single outrigger, spaced quite some distance from the hull, is bound with the same fibre, and there is not a nail or a piece of metal in the whole construction. They are strange looking craft, with their two huge, square, fibre matting sails, and they appear even stranger when you come across one far out in the ocean.

We pulled up alongside for a chat with the Tami Islander crew. The canoe was loaded with food and supplies from Lae and was bound for the Tami Islands. The canoe itself and the deck, built on the struts between the hull and the outrigger, were loaded to the gunwales with produce and cargo. She was probably moving at no more than about two knots in the light breeze, but that didn't seem to bother the crew. After a chat, they told us they expected to make landfall at Tami sometime that night. We left them and continued on our way.

After another half an hour's running, we again spotted something ahead on the horizon—another two Tami canoes also loaded to the gunwales, sailing about thirty metres apart and also heading for the Islands. We stopped again for a chat with the crews before continuing on our way.

About three and a half hours after leaving Lae, we spotted low atolls about five kilometres dead ahead. Sure enough, we had arrived at Tami. We circled round the Islands and anchored just off the beach in the lagoon near one of the villages. We discovered that this village was called Wanam, the same name as the island.

We had no tender on the *Tangimoana*, but a villager came out to us in a small canoe and gave us a lift to the beach. We spent the day looking around the village and chatting with the inhabitants. They were very friendly and quite fascinated to have a couple of white men arrive out of the ocean to visit them. The *pikininis* hung around us like a swarm of bees, stroking our hairy white skin and chatting away nineteen to the dozen.

We spent a pleasant evening eating and talking with the villagers, and later we joined everyone in greeting the arrival of the two Tami canoes that we had most recently passed at sea. We slept in a hut in the village, and the next day we explored the village of Kalal on the second island.

On the Monday morning, we prepared to leave early and head back to Lae. It had rained during the Sunday night, and the weather was turning; the wind was getting up, and more rain was expected—not a good sign!

We both felt we had to get back to Bulolo in time for work on the Tuesday morning, so we battened down the hatches, donned our life jackets for the first time since we had bought the boat, bid the Tami villagers farewell, and headed off into the weather. The swells were increasing, and we were into three to four metre seas before we knew it. It was soon starting to look a bit grim.

Jim and I discussed turning around and heading back to Tami, but by that time the islands had disappeared from sight, and the swells were so steep that to try to turn the boat around could have led to disaster. The only thing to do was to keep on running with the nose pointing directly into the swells—climbing up to each crest, dropping down the other side into the trough, and then back up again, and on and on. It was critical to keep the boat as straight as possible so that we were ninety degrees to the face of the swell. If we had swung around, even onto the quarter, we would have broached and flipped over.

Ideally, we would have headed north-northwest toward Malasiga, the closest point on the mainland some 25 kilometres away, to try to get into the lee of the swells and the wind, and then work our way west near the coast once the swells had eased. The storm had other ideas. The wind and swells were coming west-southwest from the direction of Salamaua about 110 kilometres away, and by this time we were climbing in and out of seven to eight metre swells. The driving rain had reduced visibility to a few metres. We reckoned the tops of the swells to be about fifty metres apart, and the angle on the face of each swell was getting steeper. We had no choice but to run directly into the sea, which meant that we were getting farther and farther away from the mainland coast.

Jim and I were now taking 10-minute shifts at the helm; after 10 minutes we were each so exhausted trying to hold the boat straight up and down the swells that we just lay down flat on the deck, too stuffed to even think straight. Yet ten minutes later we had to change over again. By this time, the *Tangimoana's* engine was really labouring to climb the face of the steep swells, and we had all our fingers crossed that the engine wouldn't quit on us.

The swells were now breaking on the crests, which lifted the boat almost vertical as we breached the top of each wave. We then dropped over the crest onto the back of the swell, which had become so steep that we were literally dropping into space straight off the crest and crashing down six-odd metres into the trough. We hit the bottom with such a crash and a shudder that it felt as if the boat must shake itself to bits!

One thing that added to our concern was that, as we lay spread eagled on the floor of the cabin between shifts at the helm, we could see screws turning themselves anti-clockwise out of the frames every time we crashed down into a trough. There was nothing we could do about that, so we simply had to lie there and watch them unscrewing themselves and hope to hell old Chook had used plenty of glue when he built the boat.

I don't remember how long we crashed up and down into that sea, but after what seemed like a lifetime we detected a slight swing in the wind, the rain eased a little, and the swells began to lengthen somewhat. This made the going considerably easier, and we were able to start swinging more to the northwest on a better angle to reach the mainland coast. Eventually, we were able to start quartering the swells as they continued to lengthen and reduce in height and the crests rounded off. The closer we got to the mainland, the more the sea eased as we began gaining the lee of the land.

About four hours after we had left Tami, the rain eased off, and we sighted the mainland. What a relief that was! At long last, we staggered into the harbour at Lae, totally exhausted and very grateful to be alive. We were pleased that we had actually made the trip and explored the Tami Islands, but we decided that once was probably enough!

The Ancient Mystery of the Segaya Rock Paintings

Back in Bulolo, Jim and I had heard stories about prehistoric rock paintings on the walls of some burial caves near Mumeng, about thirty kilometres from Wau on the Lae road. They were known locally as the Buang caves. This was something that we had to see!

Jim and I rounded up a group of 10 keen adventurers from Bulolo, including Ross and Pat Wylie, Neville and Di Howcroft, and Chrissie Davis who was always up for a trip into the bush. Then the lovely Helen got wind of the impending trip and insisted on tagging along as well—but she had to ask her mother first.

Helen's Mum worked at the "Freezer", which was the local supermarket. "Mum" and I had got along very well, ever since I arrived in Bulolo. So, when Helen asked her if she could go with us on the trip, Mum agreed so long as she stuck with me. She was confident that I would look out for her "baby" daughter with all due care. Yeah right! Seventeen years old, bursting with hormones, sticking out in all the right places, and always hot on my trail—I reckoned that I was the one that needed looking out for!

I did doubt the wisdom of taking Helen with us at first, as I suspected that her lack of fitness and agility might pose a bit of a challenge on the village and jungle tracks. She refused to be left behind, however, so one fine Saturday a dozen of us piled into three Land Rovers and headed for the Buangs. We took plenty of food that the girls had prepared, and the blokes supplied the necessary survival rations, which consisted largely of a carton of SP lager.

The thirty-odd kilometres to Mumeng took about an hour because of the poor state of the gravelled road. From there, we drove another hour up a rough village track toward the village of Segaya. The Land Rovers could barely get through.

At the end of the track was a simple bamboo rest-house, with a slat floor and a grass roof, where we planned to sleep the night. The next morning, we would continue on foot.

We had taken sleeping bags, and most of us got a reasonable night's rest in the shack at the end of the track, notwithstanding the hordes of mosquitoes and the lumpy, split, *limbom* palm floor that we slept on. The next morning, we ate some of the leftovers from the previous night's meal and brewed up some coffee. Then, after packing up the rest of the gear and stowing that back into the Land Rovers, we headed off on foot, up into the hills towards Segaya village. Our plan was to make the two-hour trek via Segaya village, where we would pick up a guide, and follow the Snake River until we came to some limestone cliffs that were across the other side of the river. We would have to drop down for a difficult crossing of the fast-running river and then climb up the other side via a narrow track to the caves.

We were strung out in single file along a track that went between the village gardens when we heard a blood-curdling scream from behind us. I rushed back about fifty metres to find Helen standing in the middle of the track screaming her head off with a fully grown *muruk* (cassowary) standing about five metres away from her in the *kaukau* garden, staring her straight in the eye.

An adult *muruk* can be an intimidating sight up close. It is similar to an emu in size, but with thicker, stronger legs. It was about the same height as Helen! This *muruk* was evidently a tame bird that belonged to the villagers, and it was totally fascinated by Helen and all the noise she was making. I calmed her down and spoke sternly to the *muruk*. It peered once more at Helen with its beady eyes and wandered calmly off across the *kaukau* patch in search of its breakfast. Poor Helen had thought that she was going to be the breakfast! Once she had settled down, she stuck right behind me like glue for the rest of the trip in case any other strange livestock showed an inclination toward molesting her.

At Segaya, we stopped for a chat with the locals, asked them about the caves and the rock paintings, were formally introduced to the *muruk* (which had followed us into the village, much to Helen's consternation), and collected a village entourage to guide us to our destination. This comprised one *lapun* (old man) who designated himself the guide, plus half a dozen other villagers, and about a dozen *pikininis*. A white man couldn't go anywhere in the bush in PNG without a mob of *pikininis* trotting along behind, and in front, and generally getting under foot.

We trekked for about two hours. The going was not easy, as the terrain was hilly and the walking track narrow and rough. The heat and humidity was becoming an issue for the women and the less fit among the group. Eventually, we spotted the limestone cliffs on the other side of the gulley, and we slipped and slid our way down the steep slope to the river. The villagers were very helpful and assisted Helen,

Chrissie, and the other women to cross the river and climb up the steep cliff to the caves.

It was a challenging hike, but we all made it, with the *pikininis* chattering away nineteen to the dozen and running around everywhere like little monkeys. In fact, the Pidgin word for a young boy is *manki*, even though there are no monkeys in PNG. They helped by pushing and prodding the girls up the cliff.

The caves are, in effect, shallow crevices cut into the limestone cliffs and horizontal limestone ledges under the overhanging cliff faces. The caves may have been partially excavated out by the ancients some millennia ago, or more likely they are naturally formed and scoured out by rain and water to form shallow caves. On the floor of the caves and all along the ledges there were human bones and skeletons. Some of the more complete skeletons had remnants of dried or smoked flesh still adhering to the bones while others, which appeared to be older, were bleached white and clean by age and the elements. The *lapun* explained that these were the bones of the tribal ancestors, which had been dried and smoked after death and placed up on these ledges. He told us that his ancestors had been doing this since time began. There were obviously bones deposited here from many generations.

Mummifying the dead by draining off the bodily fluids, then suspending them in a frame over a constantly smoking fire in the middle of a hut especially constructed for the purpose, was a ritual that was common among a number of PNG's more remote tribal groups. This mummification process took about 3 months. The preserved corpses were then strapped into baskets or chairs made from sticks and arrows and carried up onto high cliffs and mountains and placed in caves or on overhung ledges. Some jungle tribes placed the seated corpses up in the tops of high trees. The reason for the elevated location is because the air is drier up high and there is constant air movement and breezes which help preserve the dried flesh adhering to the bones. If the smoked corpses were left down in the villages in the valleys and lowlands, they would quickly deteriorate in the hot, humid climate.

From what I could gather from my inspection of the burial caves and talking to the *lapun*, the Segaya tribe used a similar mummifying process to preserve their dead, but these dried corpses were laid along the ledges, or inserted into crevices lying on their sides. In many cases they appeared to have been laid or stacked on top of other corpses. This stacking of corpses was no doubt due to a lack of space in the caves and on the ledges, and it is likely that skeletons were laid on top of each other to make space for more recent or more important corpses such as those of chiefs and *Sangumas*.

The purpose of the preservation and depositing of the corpses in this manner was associated with ancestor veneration and worship. The ancestors' bones, placed high in the caves above the villages, were put there to protect and guard the living from the evil spirits which abound in the living world.

Even more fascinating than the burial grounds, however, were the rock paintings on the limestone cliff walls under the overhanging rock ledges. The red ochre painted figures were truly weird and appeared at first sight to be drawings of aliens with antennae sticking out of their heads.

Then I thought that perhaps the four legged, five toed images, could have depicted an animal of some kind, although I know of no animal, past or present, that has an antenna protruding out of the top of its head. Whatever it is that they do depict, their identity remains a mystery to this day as there is nothing that I know of that resembles the figures in the rock art. The large, oversized heads and huge eyes of the figures appeared very strange indeed and made me keep thinking of aliens painted by some prehistoric people who had perhaps encountered such beings. Then there was the mystery of what looked like Maltese Crosses painted under the figures. How on earth did these fit into the overall picture?

When asked about the paintings, the *lapun* told us that they were from *"long taim bepo"* ("a time very long ago"). Further discussion with the *lapun* and other elders revealed they believe that the paintings were not done by humans or by their own ancestors, but that they originated from a time long before the Segaya people even existed. Even the oral history passed down through the tribe over the generations contains no stories of the origins of the paintings, and neither the Segaya people nor their ancestors knew how to make such paintings. They had no idea what the pictures represented or what they meant. We took plenty of photos, paid our respects to the tribal bones, and then headed back the way we had come.

Over the years, I have tried to find out more about the Segaya rock art. Although there are occasional reports of people visiting and photographing these paintings, to date I have found no further information on the likely origins of them or any estimation of their age or history. There doesn't appear to be anything similar anywhere else in PNG either.

Leke Avora, our only native machine operator at that time, snigging hoop pine thinnings with the skidder. Bulolo hoop pine plantation, 1969.

Kinoi, one of our oldest and most senior and skilled crosscutters, felling a klinkii pine. Kinoi was a Sepik elder. Watut – Bulolo ridge, 1969.

Bulolo Hospital with patients laying out on the verandah, 1969. Due to lack of airconditioning inside and the tropical heat, it was cooler out on the verandah.

Jim Riley and me on the *Tangimoana* off Kui, on the north coast, 1968.

Gobu with a turtle shell at Buso Village, 1969. Villagers welcome our arrival.

The *Tangimoana* at anchor off Jawani Island, north coast, 1969.

Me with a turtle I caught on a reef near the Longuerue Islands, 1968.

The *pukpuk* hunters with our night's catch. Kui Logging Camp, 1968

Loading *anispotera* logs onto the Baiune log barge at Kui, 1968

Tami Island trading canoe returning from Lae. Jim and I met up with these
amazing craft in the open sea on our way to the Tami Islands, 1970.

Tami trading canoes, Wanam Island, Tami Islands, 1970.

Helen's nemesis: the Segaya Village cassowary (*muruk*)
followed us back to the village, 1969.

The mysterious Segaya rock paintings, Buang Caves, 1969.

Segaya rock paintings and ancestral bones in the Buang caves. 1969

The Mission of Getting to the Mission

One long weekend in late 1967, Ike Samuels and I decided to take a trip up to the Eastern Highlands to visit the New Tribes Mission Station at Oraguti where Ike's brother, Dean, and his family were based. It was a good opportunity for me to see some of the Highlands and to go with someone who knew the road and the names of the villages along the way. We were invited to stay at the Oraguti New Tribes Mission Station and to use that as a base to explore the Lufa and Gimi districts of the Eastern Highlands.

We took off in my Holden down the road to Lae, and across the Markham River valley and the Leron plains. From there we travelled up the Kassam Pass, crossing from Morobe Province into the Eastern Highlands Province and on to Kainantu. Kainantu is the biggest town between Lae and Goroka—in fact, it's the only town. We stopped frequently en-route to take photos and talk with some of the locals about the area.

Once we had left the Lae road and headed south across the Leron Plains, practically all the *meris* were bare breasted. This wasn't an uncommon sight in the villages around the Watut and at Wau, although *meris* around Bulolo town tended to wear *meri* blouses over their *lap laps*. Once into the Highlands, however, there was rarely a *meri* blouse to be seen, and the skirts tended to be made from woven grass string.

At the top of the Kassam Pass, we came across major road works. This was the beginning of a massive construction project building the Highlands Highway from Lae to Goroka.

As we approached Kainantu, we spotted a line of about thirty natives digging a drain along the side of the road. They were all wearing red *laplaps* with black arrows on them, and they were being supervised by three uniformed native policemen wearing red berets. We figured that these must be prisoners working on a chain gang. Without thinking, I stopped and took a couple of photos of them with my 35 millimetre slide camera. As I was getting back into the car, the nearest policeman marched up to the car and advised us that we were under arrest.

This was an interesting development. Neither Ike nor I had ever been under arrest before, so this was a whole new experience. We were sternly advised that it is strictly against the law to photograph prisoners in PNG and that we would have to accompany the policeman to the police station at Kainantu. I pleaded ignorance of the law and apologised profusely, but we were told to follow the cop on his motor cycle to the police station, regardless.

Upon arrival, the policeman proceeded to write down our names and particulars, and then he told me that he was going to confiscate my camera. I did some fast talking in my best and most obsequious Pidgin and convinced him that I had only taken two photos and that I could cancel them out by cocking the frame lever, placing my hand over the lens, and pressing the shutter button.

"There you are," I told him. "I have now photographed over the two last photos so that when they are developed they will come out blank."

This apparently satisfied him. With further warnings to obey the laws of the country ringing in our ears, we duly departed and continued on our way to Goroka.

Ike had been struggling to keep a straight face during all this palaver, and once we drove out of earshot of the long arm of the law, he started laughing. Of course, all I had done was to crank the camera onto the next frame and take a photo of my hand—twice. The photos I took of the prisoners were still safely intact.

Once we had passed Kainantu, we were in the Highlands proper. The thing that surprised me most, I suppose, was that down in the lowlands and in Morobe Province the landscape was mostly jungle, interspersed with occasional villages, a few people, and scattered gardens. Up here in the Highlands, however, there was mile upon mile of *kunai* grass-covered hills, very few trees, numerous villages and gardens, and many more people.

Just before the town of Goroka, we turned left into the Lufa sub-district and really headed off the beaten track. The previously gravelled main road turned into a narrow, one-lane, dirt track. It was passable by the Holden, but only just— and only because it was the dry season, and the rutted, corrugated dirt track was rock hard.

The Holden was built for Aussie back roads and, as such, it had a high ground clearance and a crawler low gear. Some of the narrow timber bridges on the track had two or three longitudinal stringers but no lateral decking at all, so Ike and I would get out, forage around for scraps of timber and branches, and re-deck those we could with the material that we found. Sometimes we couldn't find anything to build a deck with, so we drove across on the stringers. That was a hairy exercise, to say the least! Ike would stand on the far side of the bridge and indicate a bit to the left or right as I battled to keep the wheels straight on the partly rounded surfaces of two longitudinal stringer logs!

When we could find a few planks or logs to place across the stringers as decking, there were never enough to span the entire bridge, so I would drive across as far as I could. Then Ike would pick up the planks from behind the car and place them in the front so we could use them again. The deck was barely as wide as the wheel base of the car, so Ike would walk over first and then guide me, inch by inch, across the planks. It was a bit tricky in spots, but we made it and arrived at the Oraguti New Tribes Mission Station still in one piece.

Ike and I spent three days based at the mission but spent most of that time wandering around the villages of the Gimi Valley with Dale Palmer, the head of the Oraguti Mission Station. Dale spoke the Gimi language and was a mine of information concerning the customs and culture of the Gimi people.

It was my first time in the Highlands, and I was fascinated by the significant differences between the tribal cultures of the Eastern Highlands and Morobe Province. We visited numerous Gimi villages, including Oraguti village itself, Lupabe, Forapi, Misapiberi, and Amusa. The time spent in these villages talking to the village chiefs and some of the villagers gave me invaluable insights into the customs and cultures indigenous to this part of the Eastern Highlands.

I procured some native artefacts for just a few Aussie dollars in some of the villages that we explored in the Highlands. They included a warrior's shield, bows and arrows, a *sing sing* (traditional dancing) snake belt, various shell and woven string belts and necklaces, *bilum* bags and the like. At that stage I was just collecting items that interested me, with no real pattern or aim to my collecting. I had also collected native artefacts in the Watut, Wau, Baime, and Kukukuku areas and was starting to accumulate quite a significant collection. My *donga* in Bulolo was beginning to look a bit like a museum.

Arse grass and pig grease

The cultural habits of the Eastern Highlanders were quite different from the people nearer the coast. It was much cooler up in the Highlands at over 1,500 metres above sea level, even though it was only six degrees south of the equator. As far as I could tell, few of the Highlanders ever seemed to bathe, and when the weather got a bit too cold they just rubbed another layer of pig grease onto their bodies. You can imagine the smell at a village market in the middle of a hot day. Rancid is the word that comes to mind! I did see some exceptions though, particularly among the *pikininis* and teenage *meris* who tended to swim and splash around in any stream or pool they could find.

The *meris* were almost all bare breasted, and most wore a short skirt worn to just above the knee. Some of these were made from *kunai* grass, and some were made of handmade rolled string, which was sometimes dyed with a dark coloured, natural vegetable dye. Most of them wore necklaces made of coloured beads threaded onto strings (predominantly red but sometimes yellow or blue), and small cowrie shells threaded onto handmade string worn around their waist.

The older *meris* wore large half-moon-shaped pearl shells around their necks. These were highly prized adornments and passed from mother to daughter. Many also wore numerous strings of red coloured beads around their waists like a loose belt. Some older *meris* also wore cassowary quills through their noses. These were inserted into the end of the nose from the top or tip, rather than horizontally through the septum as was the custom with the men.

All *meris* from about the age of three or four carried a woven string *bilum* bag hanging from their heads. This appeared to be the equivalent of western women carrying a handbag. Babies were carried around in a mother or sister's *bilum* or slung on the hip of an older sister.

The *mankis* and many of the older boys and men wore a string belt with a bunch of pandanus-type leaves hanging front and behind. The plant that they used for their "trousers" was grown all around the villages. The twigs of these plants each bore half a dozen individual leaves in a bunch. When they walked out of their house in the morning, the *mankis* simply broke off a couple of bunches of these leaves and tucked them into the string around their waists. The Pidgin term for this item of Highlander gentlemen's apparel is *arse grass*.

Some men and initiated boys wore a kind of loin cloth made from pounded bark or hand-made string. A common form of dress for many men was the string or bark loin cloth hanging down the front, and *arse grass* at the rear. There were a few more sophisticated gents who were dressed in more sartorial splendour. These gents' suits consisted solely of a pair of grubby cotton shorts that had never seen water (other than rain) since the owner purchased or found them.

All people of the Gimi have a reverence for pigs. The pig is the most important possession in a Gimi's life, and a man's wealth is calculated by the number of pigs he owns. A *meri* will often suckle a piglet on her own breast if it is weak or the sow can't feed it properly. Gimi *meris* will sometimes simultaneously suckle a piglet on one breast and a baby on the other. This is not uncommon throughout the Highlands.

There are two main types of houses in a Gimi village. There are the *haus b'long man* (men's houses) and the *haus b'long meri* (women's houses). The *haus b'long man* are raised on stilts and accessed by a ladder, and these are located on the higher ground in the village. The construction of these houses usually consists of woven bamboo walls, a split slat floor, and a *kunai* grass roof. The *haus b'long man* accommodates the men and the initiated boys of the village.

The *haus b'long meri* are generally circular huts with *kunai* grass roofs and vertical stick and mud walls. These are built on the ground and have a dirt floor. The eaves of the roof are about a metre off the ground, and the single door is only about 1.2 metres high. There are no windows and no chimney. A fire is always alight and smouldering in the centre of the single room, and the smoke fills the ceiling cavity until it exits out via the top of the open door. There are bamboo sleeping platforms about 30 centimetres off the ground where the *meris* and *pikininis* (and often the piglets) sleep, while the pigs sleep on the dirt floor and under the sleeping platforms. The smoke that accumulates in the ceiling area eliminates the mosquitoes and bugs. So long as you are squatting on the floor or lying on the sleeping platforms you can breathe, because these spaces are below the level of the top of the door where the smoke exits. The atmosphere inside a *haus b'long meri* reeks of smoke, rancid pig grease, and pigs.

There is a third type of house, but usually only one exists in each village.

115

This is a square house with walls of split slatted sticks, a *kunai* grass, thatched roof, and a slatted stick floor, which is raised about 2 metres off the ground. This is the boys' initiation house. The initiation of the boys in the Eastern Highlands is very elaborate and takes place gradually over many years. The boys have very little to do with their fathers until final initiation, which usually takes place at about age fourteen or fifteen among the Gimi. The boys will sleep in the *meri* houses with their mothers, siblings, and pigs until initiation, after which they will relocate to the *man* houses.

Initiation ceremonies and practices vary widely between tribal groups, but usually consist of nose-bleeding, forced vomiting, and nose-piercing, among other practices. The initiation process is to cleanse the boy of his association with women and to prepare him to ascend to the status of a man and warrior.

The space under the initiation house is reserved for pig killing ceremonies. Pigs are never killed just for day to day eating. A pig killing ceremony is a very complex process whereby hundreds of pigs are killed. I was told of one pig kill in the Gimi where 2,000 pigs were killed, and apparently that is not uncommon. Other friendly villages are invited to the feast and visiting villagers will also bring pigs for the mass killing. The meat is normally smoked and then distributed to everyone in attendance. Some of the meat is often distributed over long distances if the village doing the pig killing owes pig meat to someone quite far away. The initiation of a group of boys in a village is always accompanied by a major pig killing ceremony, and the initiates eat freshly-killed cooked pork inside their house before anyone else gets to eat. A common downside to this periodic, massive availability of pork meat which is often only partially cooked, or half smoked, is that by gorging or over-eating on the meat, many people develop what is known as *"pik bel"* or pig belly. The clinical name for *pik bel* is *necrotising enteritis* and the symptoms are demonstrated by a significant distention of the stomach often resulting in death. It is in fact the most common cause of death of children over 12 months of age in the New Guinea Highlands.

The next trip that I made to the Eastern Highlands was with Jim Riley after I had traded the Holden for a 1960 short wheel-base Land Rover. Jim and I visited some of the same villages, but also a number of different ones to those that Ike and I had explored on my previous visit. The teenage Gimi girls loved to hang around us and often hitched a ride in the Land Rover from one village to the next, just for the fun of the ride.

The Gimi people again made us very welcome, and I took the opportunity on this second trip to procure more artefacts to add to my ever-increasing collection.

The Laughing Death

It was August 1968 and another long weekend when Jim and I decided to take a further trip to the Eastern Highlands specifically to find out more about the mystery of the Forê people (pronounced "Four-ay") and the disease they called *kuru* or "the laughing death". We had heard a little about *kuru* from the anthropologists at the Bishop Museum in Wau, and we were fascinated by what appeared to be one of the strangest phenomena we had heard of in PNG. There was no such thing as personal computers or Google in those days, so if you wanted to find out about something you had to go there yourself.

We headed for the Eastern Highlands in my now lime-coloured Land Rover. En-route, we travelled through the Chimbu District, and there were so many *meris* wandering along the road that we decided that we had to photograph some of them—for ethnological and scientific purposes of course! We would stop near a group of girls and line them up. They were all most obliging, giggling a lot, and sticking their chests out for the camera. We ended up with about a dozen boxes of slides from that trip!

As fascinating as the *meris* were, however, our destination and main interest lay much further away in the interior of the Eastern Highlands—the village of Okapa and the nearby *Kuru* Research Station at Awande. The road (or rather track) to Okapa was narrow, rutted, potholed, and sometimes barely passable even in the four-wheel drive Land Rover. On numerous occasions we had to stop and search about for bits of wood and branches to lay as temporary decks across the bed logs that were all that remained of some of the bridges. We had to travel the length of the Gimi sub-district to get to Awande on the Forê border. We stopped at various villages along the way and at the Rongo Lutheran Mission Station near Lufa to ask the people we met what they could tell us about *kuru* and the Forê people in general. Yet it was not until we had spent a few days in the Forê valley and at Awande, the *Kuru* Research Station, that we were finally able to piece all the information together, separate fact from fiction, and at long last solve the mystery of *kuru* to our own satisfaction.

The natural beauty of New Guinea is something that must be experienced to be believed, from the dense tropical jungle that stretches from the coast, to the beautiful little tropical islands with white coral-sand beaches lined with coconut palms, and up into the mountains and grasslands of the Highlands. In this land of beauty and diversity, however, there are to be found examples of almost unbelievable primitiveness.

Kuru has only been known to occur in one area in the entire world: the valley of the Forê people deep in the remote mountains of the Eastern Highlands of the New Guinea mainland. This is a relatively large but very isolated valley inhabited by some 20,000 people of the Forê tribe. This tribe has its own language and ethnic culture and is virtually cut off from the rest of PNG by the high mountains all around. Even their nearest neighbours, the Gimi people, have very little direct contact with them.

The Forê tribe was only discovered in about 1945, and it was only then that the outside world came to know of the terrible "laughing death". The disease was found to be so common in the valley that the people accepted it as an inevitable part of life. *Kuru*, like all other forms of illness in the highland villages, was believed to be the direct result of sorcery and magic and was, therefore, accepted with resignation.

One of the strangest things about *kuru* was that it was found to occur almost exclusively among the women and children of the tribe. It ran a predictable course, the initial stages of which produced occasional loss of control of the emotions and physical stability. The victim, in the first month of infection, would suddenly burst out laughing or crying for no apparent reason and generally exhibit violent changes of emotion. After about three months, the victim would be unable to fully control their limbs and would often fall over or begin twitching. After about six months, the final stage would set in when the affected person could no longer control their emotions or nervous system at all, and they were then unable to feed themselves. Their uncontrollable, hysterical laughter would go on continuously day and night, until about the ninth month when the victim would die. Death occurred from a mixture of exhaustion, starvation, and the internal effects of *kuru*. The disease always followed the same pattern and was always fatal within nine months.

In 1950, an American medical investigation team under the leadership of Dr Carl Gajdusek set up the Kuru Research Station at Awande, near Okapa, which is near the southern end of the Forê Valley. For twenty years, the station was manned by research staff coming to stay and study for a few months each year in an effort to trace the cause of the disease and hopefully to find a cure.

Kuru was one of the biggest mysteries in PNG for many years. Here was a disease found only in this one place, 100 percent fatal, affecting primarily women and children, and with no obvious cause. Large numbers of the tribe died each year—some years the death rate was reportedly as high as 2,000!

To counteract this depletion of the female population, every couple of years the men of the tribe would make raiding excursions on nearby tribes (predominantly the neighbouring Gimi) and take significant numbers of women and children back to the Forê Valley as replacements. Strangely, these imported women only rarely contracted the disease.

In the PNG Highlands, especially among the more isolated tribes, the incidence of cannibalism was very real at that time (and in some places still is) and quite common, as it has been since time immemorial for these people. In days gone by, before government patrols and missionaries gained some measure of control, it was quite common for inter-tribal warfare to result in cannibalistic feasts where the bodies of those slain in battle were eaten by the conquering tribe. The general belief was that by eating the bodies of the enemy, the victors would inherit the strength of the victim in addition to their own.

In many areas of the country, however, especially in the Highlands where the bulk of the population live, cannibalism was the only method of obtaining much needed protein. There are very few native mammals in the New Guinea Highlands, and the people have always been starved of protein. Even now, there is very little protein available except for domestic pigs, which hardly count as they are only killed on ceremonial occasions.

In more modern times, since the killing of other tribes has been discouraged by the missionaries and the administration, it has become necessary to find an alternative way of obtaining protein. There was only one immediately available and obvious solution. There was always someone in the tribe dying of something or other, and it was certainly a waste of good protein to bury them in the ground, stack them in burial caves, or prop them up in trees, so why not be practical and eat them? Consequently, it became common among the more primitive tribes (mainly those in the Highlands), to hold a brief period of mourning for the deceased—usually only a few hours or a day or two—and then proceed with the business of cooking and eating them. This meat was usually eaten with fire-baked *kaukau* and yams.

This is still not an uncommon practice, even today. My own visits to *"kuru* country" were in the 1970s, but my knowledge of 21st century PNG tells me that little has changed in many more remote areas, even though the present administration may throw up its hands in horror and officially deny it.

There is a strong belief among the people of the Highlands that certain organs (brains, heart, liver, and kidneys) hold special strengthening properties. In the days of inter-tribal warfare, these organs were always given to the warriors to give them greater strength in battle. In later times though, it became more common to give these delicacies to the women and children in order that they became stronger (and, in the women's case, better able to breed) and to do all the menial work their society demands of them.

The Forê people were no exception when it came to protein requirements and cannibalism. They did, however, practice one major variation from all the other tribes. The ethnic beliefs of the Forê tribes, based exclusively on sorcery, magic, witchcraft, and superstition, held that when a member of the tribe died, he or she must be mourned for a period of up to 24 hours, then the body must be buried in the ground for a period of three to four weeks in order that the spirit could successfully leave the body. After that period, it was believed that the body was devoid of all spiritual attachment. It was then dug up, cleaned, cooked, and eaten. The brains, liver, heart, and kidneys were given to the women and children.

It was eventually discovered by Gajdusek's research team, following years of painstaking work and through the process of successfully infecting a chimpanzee with *kuru*, that while the body was buried in the ground, a virus developed inside the brain and liver. When these parts were eaten by the women and children, the virus was passed on to them. The virus lived and bred in the new host and infected the brain and the nervous system, thereby producing *kuru* and eventually a certain death. The reason that the imported women from other tribes seldom succumbed to the disease was that they were naturally reluctant to eat the partially decomposed flesh.

In the late 1970s, the emphasis of the research team's efforts changed to education of the Forê people as to the cause of *kuru*, and efforts were made to stop the cannibalistic practice. This, however, is not as simple as it sounds. Firstly, if they stopped eating human flesh, where would they obtain an alternative source of protein? Who was going to supply 20,000 people with a supply of meat or other protein indefinitely? If someone did that, then they would also have to supply meat to the remainder of the two million odd people of the Highlands. These people have no money to buy meat and no means of earning any. The Forê will not be dissuaded from their practices of funerary cannibalism because of their inbred culture and fear of sorcery.

There is virtually no government control in the Forê valley and no resident missionary groups within their borders. Consequently, there was little difference between the Forê people of 100 years ago and the Forê people of the 1970s, although it has been reported that in the early 2000s the incidence of the disease was slowly reducing as the older people were dying out.

The *Kuru* Research Station at Awande (at least from the late 1960s) helped to care for the dying women and children who contract the disease and assisted in caring for some of the uninfected children of the victims. It is unlikely that a cure will ever be found for *kuru*. Recent reports, however, indicate that *kuru* is now definitely on the decline and may by now even have been eliminated entirely.

The Islands of Love and Yams

One weekend in 1970, a group of us decided to make the trip from Bulolo to the Trobriand Islands. The Trobriand Islands are a group of islands off the eastern tip of the PNG mainland. They are known as "the Islands of Love" because of the peculiar male/female relationship arrangements endemic to these islands. The Trobriand Islands are a matriarchal society, and the courtships and most activities leading up to them are instigated as much by the girls as the boys.

The Trobriands consist of four main islands, the largest and by far the most populous being Kiriwina which is the location of the only airstrip and was our destination. Kiriwina is about 40 kilometres long and contains some 60 villages with a total population of around 10,000 people

Sex and intimate relationships are free and easy and commence at a relatively young age. Although an understanding of reproduction and modern medicine is now relatively widespread in Trobriand society, the Islanders' traditional beliefs have endured and the cause of pregnancy is still largely blamed on a *baloma* (a local spirit). It is believed that the *baloma* is inserted into, or enters the body of the woman, and this is the reason that a woman becomes pregnant. In the past this traditional belief endured because the yam, the major food and form of exchange on the islands, incorporates significant contraceptive properties, so the practical link between sex and pregnancy was never very evident.

Trobriand children begin to play erotic games with each other at about age seven or eight, imitating the adults. At about age twelve both boys and girls begin to pursue sexual partners. They change partners often, and the girls are just as assertive as the boys in pursuing a lover.

When a Trobriand couple decide to marry, they demonstrate their intention by sleeping with each other and spending time together. If, after a year, a wife is unhappy with her husband, she may divorce him. A couple may also get divorced if the husband chooses another woman. If the man decides to go back to his original wife, he demonstrates this by giving yams to her family, but it is ultimately up to the woman herself if she wants to return to him. Woman's lib may well have been invented in the Trobriand Islands!

My fellow expats and I had heard these stories about the Trobriands, so we decided that we should go down and check them out. We organised a group to go from Bulolo and chartered an old DC3 out of Lae. The DC3 landed at the Bulolo airstrip about seven a.m. on the Saturday morning. We boarded the passengers, loaded a few cartons of SP in case of emergencies, and away we went.

It was a perfect morning weather-wise, and we enjoyed a great low-level scenic flight from Bulolo over the jungle to Salamaua on the north coast. We followed the coast to the eastern tip of the mainland and then flew across the ocean until Kiriwina Island came into sight.

We spent a fascinating weekend wandering around Kiriwina and talking to the villagers. There was a rustic guest house that had recently been built near the main village on Kiriwina, and we had arranged to stay there for the night. The food at the hotel was fairly basic but OK, but the SP beer was cold, which was the most important thing. The weather was very hot and humid, so the young *mankis* were kept gainfully occupied climbing coconut trees and throwing down green coconuts for us to drink.

The Islanders are skilled wood carvers, and there were plenty of traditional carvings available for sale at very cheap prices. They used mainly a native red cedar and black ebony wood for their carvings. Popular souvenirs, especially among the ladies of the group, were the various sized fish-shaped dishes and small nesting tables with carved legs. Some of us also purchased Trobriand grass skirts, which are made from a local grass grown for that purpose, and also from shredded and dried banana leaves. They are dyed with locally made vegetable dyes.

Yams grow very well on the coral soils of the islands. These are not only an important part of the Islanders' diet; they are also used for trade, gifts, and exchange. There is even an annual yam eating festival, a very important occasion on the calendar in the Trobriands. The islanders build tall, highly decorated structures for storing yams throughout the year. Even in 1970 when we visited, a man's importance was gauged by the height, size, and decoration of his yam store.

The Trobriand Islanders appeared to be a pleasant ethnic mixture of Melanesian and Polynesian, some with a dash of missionary thrown in, I suspect. As such, I found them to be much more attractive looking people than your average Papua New Guinean. Most of us blokes were gainfully occupied ogling the pretty Trobriand Island girls dressed in their short, colourful grass skirts, and not much else.

I found the Trobriand Islanders a very clean people who bathe daily and are very particular about their appearance—very different from the New Guinea Highlanders! The water for the villages that we visited came from fresh water springs located at various places on the island. The women and girls bathe and wash their clothes at the spring, then carry drinking water back to the house in gourds or large round bowls balanced on their heads.

Some of us were wandering about down by the mangroves thinking about going for a swim when we spotted a couple of huge monitor lizards in the mangrove trees. We then noticed the fresh footprints of a large salt-water crocodile and decided then that perhaps we wouldn't go swimming after all. Yet we came around a corner in the creek, and here was a bunch of little *pikininis* swimming and poling dugout canoes around the estuary and having a great old time! We asked the kids if they weren't worried about the crocodiles, but they just laughed. We asked a nearby fisherman in a canoe about the crocs, and he told us that ten people had been eaten by crocodiles around there in the past year!

The Remarkable Mr Foad

In early 1969, a friend based in Wau asked Jim and I if we wanted to fly to Nugidu near Finschhafen for the weekend and meet up with an old New Guinea legend by the name of Ted Foad. We were keen to go, as we had been discussing trying to get to Finschhafen for some time, and we had heard stories about Ted Foad. Until now, however, we had been stymied because the only way that we knew of to get to Finschhafen was by sea—a long haul up the coast from Lae.

Our mate, Mike Tuohy, was a Morobe District *Kiap* (Patrol Officer). He was the son of Austin Tuohy who was then High Commissioner for Morobe Province. Mike had his own Cessna 170 bush plane, a light, single engine, four-seater, tail-wheel aircraft favoured by bush pilots because of its very short landing and take-off capabilities. This solved the problem of getting to Finschhafen, so we agreed to join him and his friend Klaus Stromblad, who was visiting Mike in Wau at the time.

Finschhafen is a small town located some 80 kilometres east of Lae on the Huon Peninsula. Finschhafen port was discovered by Europeans in 1884 by the German researcher Otto Finsch. In 1885 the German colony of New Guinea created a town on the site and named it after the discoverer. Evangelical Lutheran missionaries settled near the town, establishing a Mission station at Simbang and later at Sattelberg approximately three miles away.

Malaria was the big problem for the settlers from the start. An epidemic in 1891 caused the colonists to briefly leave, only to return and then leave again ten years later in 1901. During the Second World War, Finschhafen was fought over by Japan, Australia, and the United States because of its strategic position along the north coast.

Most of the original houses were destroyed during the war, and the town was re-developed somewhat further away near the military airport built by the Japanese. The Finschhafen airport itself was established as an important base for the US Army.

At the war's end, millions of dollars' worth of equipment such as trucks, Jeeps, and planes, both new and used, were bulldozed into huge holes dug in the area or dumped into the sea and abandoned. Aircraft, ammunition, and various metals such as brass and bronze were recovered and smelted after the war for great profits, a good proportion of it recovered by Ted Foad. There are many rumours and facts about caches of buried equipment that yet remain in the jungle. Over the decades, numerous aircraft or partial wrecks, which were either abandoned at the Finschhafen airfield, partially or completely buried, or bulldozed into the sea, have been salvaged from this location.

Early on the Saturday morning, Mike and Klaus landed at Bulolo where they collected Jim and me, and we took off for Finschhafen. The old Nugidu airstrip is about 16 kilometres north of Finschhafen, located along the narrow Nugidu Peninsular between the ocean and the Nugidu lagoon. There was a small sandy beach with some overhanging trees down at the end, and you could see the old Lutheran mission house on the side of the hill opposite.

The airstrip is about 600 metres long, and at the top end, furthest from the ocean, there is a tin shed that passes for the terminal building. This shed was within walking distance of Ted's house and buildings, which formed the base for his business retrieving wartime salvage. He also owned a small aircraft charter business.

Apparently, the whole area of the Nugidu Peninsular was cleared during the Second World War and used to store supplies and equipment offloaded from ships. The Nugidu airstrip was built not long after the war using *coronos* (crushed coral rock). The *coronos* was tarred with asphalt at some stage, although it was very dilapidated, potholed, and overgrown when we landed on it.

We flew in low over the islands and coral reefs off the Nugidu Peninsular and then did two low runs along the strip at near stalling speed, a few feet off the deck, to see what the surface was like. The strip didn't look like it had been used for a long time, as the asphalt surface was all broken up with huge pot holes everywhere, and big clumps of kunai grass and weeds grew all over it. Mike reckoned he had landed on it a couple of times over the past few years when he was patrolling in the area. He also knew Ted Foad, who was the man we had come to meet.

Mike picked out a short section of runway that looked a bit better than the rest and dropped the Cessna down onto the deck, dodging some of the bigger potholes and grass clumps. We taxied up to the tin shed at the end, which probably once constituted some sort of airport shelter. In the nearby lagoon was a half-sunken Japanese patrol boat sticking out of the mud, and the remains of the old wartime wharves. There was also an old, ex-army Patrol Torpedo (PT) crash boat tied up in the lagoon with a smaller launch moored behind it. These last two belonged to Ted whose house and sheds were only a short walk from where we parked the plane.

Ted Foad was originally from England and he travelled to Australia at a young age, and then carried on to New Guinea to join his father's fishing business. Ted eventually acquired his own boat and began trading in copra. He later took up gold prospecting, often working in remote uncontrolled locations. When the war started in the Pacific, Ted joined the New Guinea Volunteer Reserve, but he was soon back in small ships supplying the forces around the New Guinea coast.

After the war, Ted built up a coastal transport business and in the 1960s started a helicopter business to service the goldfields. In all, Ted spent 41 years living and working in New Guinea.

The compound surrounding Ted's house seemed to be full of chickens and naked *pikininis*. Ted came out to greet us as we wandered into the compound, and we sat down on an old torpedo and had a cup of tea (as you do), brewed up by one of the *meris* who appeared to be part of Ted's entourage.

Ted was a really interesting character. Here he was, apparently worth the odd zillion, dressed in a pair of crusty old shorts and bare feet, living out there in the New Guinea jungle with no road to anywhere, and surrounded by chickens, *pikininis*, *meris*, and dodgy looking torpedoes. It wasn't clear if all or any of the three or four *meris* and the umpteen snotty-nosed *pikininis* belonged to Ted. Maybe he had adopted a whole tribe.

Ted told us about how, among other things, he had been collecting scrap metal for years from left-over war machinery and munitions, sorting it, and selling it. He had set up collection points at villages along the coast and up the rivers and inlets where the Americans, Japanese, and Australians had left equipment and ammunition behind when the Second World War ended. The local villagers would locate the stuff he wanted, especially brass, bronze, ammunition, radiators, and whatever, then they would drag it out of the bush and down to a collection point on the coast. He would motor up in his PT Crash Boat, his crew would load the collected scrap onto the boat, he would pay the locals off, and then they would return back into the jungle to search for more.

The Yanks had also pushed heaps of brand new Jeeps, trucks, and even aircraft off barges into the sea off the coast of Finschhafen at the end of the war. Ted had local divers recover anything from these watery scrap-heaps that was in water shallow enough to be accessed by them.

Ted had acquired the 80-foot long Elco PT Crash Boat as surplus after the war. He had stripped out the three original Packard 1,200 hp, turbo-charged, aero petrol engines that were so powerful that the hulls needed special strengthening to support them, and he replaced these with two 300 hp diesel engines. To operate the boat using the original gas-gobbling Packard petrol engines, he would have needed a petrol tanker to follow along behind him.

During the war the original Crash Boat setup sported six mufflers on the transom, one for each bank of six cylinders. When it was time to operate under stealth, the crews muffled the engines. When it was time to get out and go for it, they removed the mufflers and ran on 4-inch straight pipes fixed directly off the exhaust manifolds. The un-muffled racket of 3,600 hp at full noise must have been incredible!

These PT boats were built of triple layered plywood, uncoated with fibreglass or anything else. It required over a million screws to plank an Elco hull. They were tremendously fast and strong boats. Ted's ex-PT boat we had seen parked in the lagoon was named the *Beringa*. He said that he didn't use it much these days, as he had cleaned out most of the readily available scrap from up the coast. Now he had arrangements with the villagers around the area to collect any of the more valuable stuff that they could find, or dig up, or dive for, and bring it directly to him. This included ammunition of all kinds, brass, copper, radiators, propellers, etc. The local people would transport it to Ted's place in their canoes and sell it to him.

Ted had some big corrugated iron sheds on the edge of the lagoon, about 80-odd metres away from the house. These were his storage and processing sheds. Inside were enough shells and ammunition to start a small war! There were machine gun bullets, .303 bullets by the truckload, big anti-aircraft shells, and scrap metal of all kinds, along with trochus shells, copra, and coffee. Ted bought this scrap and product from the local people and then sorted it all, semi-processed some of it—such as the ammo—and sold it when he had sufficient to make a boat load. Ted had also accumulated an incredible collection of catalogued sea shells, some of them very rare, and he proudly showed them to us.

There were old torpedoes lying around outside his house and on the edge of the lagoon. While sitting on one having lunch, I asked Ted if they were still live. He reckoned he didn't know for certain, and he certainly wasn't going to open them up to find out.

Our attention was caught by a lot of tapping and banging going on in the big shed nearest the lagoon. When we asked about it, Ted offered to give us the guided tour. Inside the shed were two long work benches running the length of the shed and facing each other. At about 2 metre intervals there was a vice bolted to the bench. Under the bench were 44-gallon drums cut in half, placed side by side, with one positioned directly under each vice. Along the benches were piles of live .303 bullets and other ammunition. Working at a couple of the vices were local natives, each equipped with a hammer and a pair of modified pliers. The worker would pick up a bullet, place it in the vice with the projectile end up, tighten the vice, twist out the copper jacketed, lead projectile with the pliers, and toss that into one of the drums. Then he would reverse the cartridge so that the open end pointed down into the drum which was positioned under the vice. He would whack the percussion end with a wooden mallet so that the cordite (a smokeless "gunpowder") fell into the drum. While the now empty cartridge case was still in the vice, he would knock out the percussion cap with a hammer and what looked like a sharpened screwdriver. The percussion caps were placed into containers on the bench, and the empty shell cases were tossed into a third drum.

It was certainly an efficient system of separating and sorting the various components of a cartridge. Like most cunning plans, however, there was one drawback inherent in the system. Much of the ammo had been buried for years in the ground or under water, and the cordite inside some of the shells had become damp and sticky. When we asked Ted about what had taken the chunks out of some of the benches, and what had made the big hole in the tin roof above one of the vices, he said, "yeah, well about that....". He then explained that about a year ago he had handed over the business of disassembling the cartridges to his local workers and paid them for the lead and brass they produced. Unfortunately, they sometimes got a bit careless and when Ted returned from a trip to Australia one time, he was a bit miffed to find a couple of big holes in the side of his shed and one through the roof.

Ted noted that sometimes the old cordite might be a bit sticky and didn't always fall out into the drum, leaving some—or even all of it, still in the case. Occasionally, the guy working on a sticky shell belted the percussion cap a bit too hard, or at the wrong angle, which accidently detonated the cap and caused the wad of cordite and an accompanying spark to fire straight down into the partly-full cordite drum under the bench. The cordite drums were supposed to be regularly emptied so they didn't contain too much cordite at any one time in case a spark did shoot down. This was so that in the event this happened, then there wouldn't be much to ignite. On the odd occasion, however, a spark shot straight into a half-full drum of cordite, which then exploded with an almighty bang! On more than one occasion, the drum, its entire contents, part of the bench and the vice, exited straight up through the roof and were possibly mistaken for New Guinea's first attempt to launch a satellite! On the last occasion that this happened, the guy working at the vice also disappeared never to be seen again. It's not sure if he went up through the roof with the vice or whether he got such a fright he took to his scrapers and disappeared into the jungle—in which case he may still be running to this day.

There was a road of sorts from Ted's place to the mission station, the TB (tuberculosis) hospital, and Finschhafen town. Ted gave us a ride in his beat-up Land Cruiser ute to have a look at the old mission and the minaret falls on the Finsch River. These waterfalls were quite beautiful, with a natural swimming pool at the base. There were some young *meris* bathing in the pool and a dozen or so *pikininis* splashing around. They screamed their heads off with excitement when they spotted us. If these falls were anywhere else in the world and had road access, they would become a major tourist attraction.

We stayed the night at Ted's house, and the *meris* cooked us up a good feed while we supplied a carton of tinned pineapple slices and a box of SP that we had brought with us. We spent a great evening with Ted, who regaled us with yarns of his life and exploits in the New Guinea jungle, and around the coast. Ted Foad was a genuine PNG character whom it was indeed a pleasure and a privilege to meet.

Chimbu *meris* near Chuave, Chimbu District, August 1968.

Prisoners working on the chain gang, Kainantu, 1967. This is the infamous
photo that had me arrested!

Me posing with some friendly Gimi *meris*. Eastern Highlands, 1968.

Gimi beauties at Oraguti village, Eastern Highlands, 1968.

Gimi *manki* wearing "*arse grass*", a key item of Highlander gentlemen's apparel.
Near Oraguti, Eastern Highlands, 1969.

Chimbu *meri* breast-feeding a piglet and a *pikinini* (child). Eastern Highlands, August 1968.

Haus b'long meri (women's house), where we slept the night. Dale Palmer at right.
Misapiberi village, Eastern Highlands, 1967.

Forê men encountered near the Gimi-Forê border, Eastern Highlands. They had just walked for five days to reach the Gimi border, August 1968.

The chief's yam house, Trobriand Islands, 1970. Even when I visited, a man's importance was gauged by the height, size, and decoration of his yam store.

Trobriand Island girls, 1970.

Trobriand Islands *meri* carrying water gourds to the village spring, 1970.

Nugidu Airstrip, near Finschhafen, 1969. Nugidu Lagoon on the right.

Me, Jim Riley and Mike Tuohy with Mike's Cessna at the
Nugidu terminal, 1969.

Sitting on one of Ted's "deck chairs", an old torpedo that may have still been live. Sunken Japanese patrol boat can be seen in the lagoon behind me. Nugidu, 1969.

Jim Riley (left) and Mike Tuohy with some of Ted Foad's collection of bullets and shell Nugidu, 1969.

The Fidel Castro of New Britain Island

At the end of 1970, I packed up my gear and my PNG artefact collection and returned to New Zealand. I spent 1971 working for Fletcher Forests at Tauhara near Taupo. Late in 1971, I crated up my collection of PNG artefacts and took them down to the Dominion Museum in Wellington, where I deposited them with Roger Neich, the Curator of Pacific Ethnology, under a loan agreement.

Nineteen seventy one was a busy year for me. In my spare time I learned to fly single engine aircraft and got my private pilot's licence. I also shot a lot of deer, mainly in Tauhara Forest. I often drove around the forest roads and tracks very early in the morning, when I spotted any number of big, red deer grazing in the clearings. I wasn't allowed to carry a rifle in my Landrover during the working hours of the forest when there were loggers and trucks operating, but outside working hours—well that was a different matter.

By the end of 1971 I had had enough of New Zealand, and I applied to return to PNG as a District Forest Officer (DFO) with the PNG Department of Forests.

In January 1972, I flew to Rabaul on the northern tip of New Britain Island and reported to the District Forestry Office. Once I had been briefed on my responsibilities as the new DFO for the Central North Coast of West New Britain Island, I boarded a Twin Otter aircraft and flew down the north coast to Bialla, where the Ewasse Government administration station was located between the Bialla airstrip and Nantabu village.

On disembarking I was met by Robin Brown, the local area *Kiap*, who was driving the sole government vehicle at Ewasse—an IH farm tractor towing a large trailer! I climbed onto the trailer with my backpack containing all my possessions and was dropped off at the local government council *Kiap's donga*, which was where I would be staying until I had built my own accommodation.

The local government council *Kiap* was an Aussie called Bruce. He was about the same age as me, and a good bloke. Bruce (like Robin) was away in the jungle on patrol most of the time, visiting villages and local council houses, and advising on and dispensing justice as necessary among the villagers.

There are seven major tribes in West New Britain, the largest of which are the Nakanai and the Kove. People from West New Britain are widely referred to as "Kombes" in reference to the Kove (or Kombe) tribe. The Kombes are noted especially for their practice of super-incision of the penis.

Super-incision is a practice where the foreskin is cut dorsally in a longitudinal pass of the razorblade as part of secret initiation ceremonies for male adolescents. Super-incision is generally referred to among Papua New Guineans as "the Kombe cut".

I quickly settled into the Ewasse government station environment and got to know the residents. This didn't take very long, as the expatriate residents consisted only of Robin, Bruce, and a Dutchman called Hendrick who was the *Didiman* (District Agricultural Officer). I had a good look around the surrounding area, which included Nantabu village and a native trade store that was located along the track between Ewasse and the Lebanese logging camp. The trade store was owned and operated by a Dalmatian named Branko, who was married to a local Nakanai *meri*. There was also a more up-market trade store belonging to the Lebanese logging camp a few kilometres along the coast, which stocked some expat-type produce.

I needed to build myself a house, so I arranged to have some timber, cement, and corrugated iron shipped up from Kimbe, the main government supply station located some distance down the coast near Cape Hoskins. I recruited a couple of native builders from Kimbe, who travelled up on the government supply boat with the building materials. I gave them a hand with the building from time to time, and I designed a septic tank—a large hole dug out the front of the house and lined with concrete. I built it from memory having watched Dad build septic tanks in Okato when I was a kid. I recalled that he always threw a dead possum or a hedgehog or two into a new septic tank to start the bacteria working before the doings started going in. Any such animals would be on the menu in PNG, so instead I paid the local village kids to catch some toads and frogs in the local swamp. They flattened them with lumps of wood and threw them into the tank. It must have worked, because I never smelled anything bad coming from that septic tank once it was operational.

I was responsible for monitoring and reporting on eight independent logging operations along the central north coast, but the only one that I could get to by road was the Pacific Lumber operation. This was the largest logging concession of the eight. The Pacific Lumber logging camp and its Lebanese owner's housing compound were located a few kilometres north of Nantabu, and it was connected to the coast by a single main logging road that branched into the jungle to the various operational logging areas.

Ewasse is located about midway up the west coast of New Britain Island, and there were no connecting roads at all in the area. The only roads were the local logging roads, which connected each logging area to the beach, and some walking and motorcycle tracks connecting some of the native villages. To get to the Pacific Lumber logging area, I initially borrowed the *Kiap's* tractor when it was available. This vehicle was mainly used to fetch supplies from the trade stores and to carry cargo and personnel to and from the airstrip when the planes came in.

Pacific Lumber was owned by a consortium comprising Shin Asahigawa, a Japanese log-trading company, and a Lebanese family from Melbourne, Australia. The head of the Lebanese family managing the operation was a way-out, larger-than-life character named Farid Wakim. Farid was a short, broad, stocky gent with a bushy black beard who always wore a green safari suit, a kepi-style cap, and had a big cigar sticking out of his mouth. In fact, he looked, acted, and dressed exactly like Fidel Castro (which was probably the plan), except that Farid was a bit shorter than Castro. He drove an open green Jeep with no windscreen, windows, doors, or roof, and with a gun scabbard strapped to the outside of the vehicle. The scabbard always contained an expensive looking, engraved, semi-automatic shotgun. He mostly roared around the place in his Jeep, abusing everyone loudly in Lebanese and very bad Pidgin. I was occasionally invited to Farid's big house up on the hill, where I enjoyed

141

the results of some excellent Lebanese cooking and sampled some of his cognac. It was pretty tough, but someone had to do it!

Farid had a resident entourage of extended family living at the camp. I won't say "working", as most of the cousins and uncles did bugger-all and knew nothing about logging or the New Guinea jungle, although one of the cousins, who was the cook at the Pacific Lumber cookhouse, did a pretty good job and could knock up some half-decent Lebanese tucker! The Ewasse government station residents occasionally went over to Bialla on the tractor and had dinner there. Although the cook's favourite chicken dishes were tasty and certainly much better than my own amateur culinary efforts, they were always floating in a sea of olive oil and covered in lashings of garlic. This type of cuisine was all new and foreign to me and took a while to get used to!

The Perils of Getting Dinner

One of my major missions was keeping an eye on what logs were actually being produced from the bush, what was being shipped, and the actual species and volumes of each species (compared to the records that were being declared to the Forestry Department for the payment of royalties!). All the operators had opportunities to bend the system by declaring higher volumes of low value species but cutting and shipping high value species. Under-measuring for the Forestry Department records, compared to the actual volume shipped, was something that I always had to watch out for.

I was having trouble getting to the other seven logging operations without my own transport, as I was totally dependent on hitching a ride with one of the *Kiaps* or Hendrik the *Didiman* on the one and only government speed-boat if they happened to be going my way. This proved to be quite impractical, so I hitched a ride on the government supply boat for the overnight trip to Rabaul and went to have a chat with my boss. The Forestry Department didn't have any funds available at the time to supply me with transport, so I did a deal with them whereby I would buy a boat with an outboard motor, and a small motorbike, and the Forestry Department would pay me a monthly hire rate for them. I bought a little Yamaha 100cc motor bike in Rabaul and rode it out to the Bainings some 32 kilometres further down the north coast to go and see my old mate Peter Woolcott who used to live at Bulolo.

Since I had departed Bulolo, Peter had left the Forestry Department and retired with his wife to their coconut plantation in the Bainings. Peter used to be the *lik-lik* doctor for the Forestry Department in Bulolo and was still doctoring to the locals around the Bainings. Peter was born in Australia but had lived most of his life in PNG. He had married a Tolai lady from the Bainings area, and they had two lovely daughters who were then at university in Australia.

I figured if Peter didn't have a spare boat of some sort, then he would surely know someone who did. Fortunately, he did have spares among his half a dozen vessels, and he was happy to part with one. The one that suited me best was a 14-foot fibreglass dinghy, which had started life as a centre-board yacht. The centre-board hole was glassed over, and the boat had a 28 hp Evinrude outboard hanging off it. It looked a good, sound, solid vessel, although a bit on the narrow side. Peter also had a big, old, hand-operated winch, suitable for hauling a boat out of the water, which he offered to me. We did a deal, and Peter delivered the winch and dinghy up to Rabaul for me where they and the motorbike were loaded onto the government supply boat for transport to Bialla.

When my gear arrived and was off-loaded at Bialla, I got my forestry *bois t*o cut down a couple of old coconut trees, and we dragged them to the beach in front of the compound with the *Kiap's* tractor. We set them up to form a set of rails about a metre apart, running from the beach up to the top of the bank, which was about four metres high. The coconut logs were positioned at about a 45 degree angle. We set up the winch at the top of the coconut rails and secured it to a standing coconut tree.

Once the tide came in, I hooked up my new boat to the winch cable, cranked the big handle, and hauled the dinghy up the coconut rails until the nose was sticking up above the top of the bank. The stern and the outboard were then well clear of the water at high tide, even if the water was choppy. To launch her, I first had to wait for the tide to come in, then I released the winch, and the boat slid down the rails into the water. I found some old axle grease under the *Kiap's* house and smeared some of that onto the logs, which made it easier to haul the boat in and out. If it was low tide when I returned home, then I just threw the anchor out and walked home across the flats. When the tide came in, I waded out, hauled the boat up to my coconut log slipway, and winched it out of the water again.

Now that I was fully mobile and independent, I could throw my motor bike into the boat and cruise up the coast to inspect the remaining seven of my logging operations. I ran the boat up onto the beach, unloaded the bike, and rode it up the logging road into the jungle to where the logger was operating. I had a chat with the boss and then checked, sample-measured, and recorded the logs on the bush log landings. I then went to find my native Forest Rangers, a couple of whom were based at each operation to monitor the felling operations and logging boundaries, and I checked their recording books against my own observations. When I was satisfied that everything was up to scratch, I headed back to the beach to measure and record any newly delivered logs that had been stacked ready for loading when the log ship arrived. I then loaded my bike back into my boat and continued up the coast to the next operation.

Each operation was managed by one expatriate Aussie owner and his wife, living in a simple bush house that they had built in the jungle. They employed a number of native loggers, a few of whom were Sepiks and the rest of whom were recruited from the nearby villages. Their equipment usually consisted of one bulldozer, a log skidder, a log loader, and a logging truck, as well as a Land Cruiser pickup truck, and a 14-foot aluminium dinghy with an outboard motor. When all the logging operations on the coast had combined enough logs for a ship-load, the log ship would arrive and anchor off the beach, starting at the northern-most operation and working its way down the coast. When the ship arrived, the contractor would bring his entire crew down to the beach, together with his skidder and front-end loader. The loader would have already stacked the logs that had been carted down to the beach by the logging truck. The skidder then rolled the logs into the water, and the crew lashed them into small rafts using ropes and wire strops. When they had six to eight logs rafted up together, the dinghy would tow them out to the waiting ship where they would be secured alongside and loaded using the ship's cranes. When the logs from one operation were all loaded, the ship would move on down the coast to the next operation.

As soon as I had finished my rounds each day, I headed back home, running along the outer edge of the coral reefs. I towed a lure out the back on the return journey, and I usually caught a couple of giant trevally, tuna, or other good eating fish. Sometimes I would cruise in among the shallow reefs, find a good spot in about one or two metres of water, throw out the anchor, don my goggles, snorkel and flippers, and poke around under the flat, umbrella coral heads to catch me a couple of crayfish. Once I had caught enough for a feed, I headed home, winched the boat up, and sat under the coconut palms with a cold SP lager, discussing the day's activities and swapping yarns with the *Kiap* or the *Didiman*. It was a pretty good life for a young forest ranger, and it suited me just fine.

One afternoon, I had been diving along the edge of a reef attempting to catch a few crayfish to share around the camp. At one stage, I had to reverse fairly rapidly out of a hole to evade a black and white banded coral snake that had made its home under the coral head! I had caught four good crays and was heading back across the reef towards my boat, towing my string with the crayfish attached, when I spotted some feelers waving about from under a big umbrella coral. I decided to swim around and under the umbrella head to catch the crayfish by surprise before they reversed too far under for me to reach them. I was working my way around when I felt a tug on the cord that I was towing. Thinking that I had snagged one of my tethered crayfish on an antler coral, I tried to pull it free. Suddenly the rope went taut, and something started to drag me backwards! That was a bit of a worry, so I put my snorkel up for air and turned around to see what the problem was.

Hanging off the end of the cord and firmly holding onto the crayfish that I had tied at the end of the line was a two metre long reef shark! He was sedately cruising off across the reef with my crayfish in his mouth. I was understandably annoyed about this, as I didn't want to lose my hard-earned catch, so I gave the rope a good jerk to try to dissuade him in his endeavours and make him let go of my lunch. He wasn't too interested in that option, however, and continued to swim away. So, I went down onto the reef feet first, jammed my flippers behind a big coral outcrop, and gave the rope a really hard yank. The crayfish in the shark's mouth broke apart, and bits of it drifted into water around him. Fortunately, his point of concentration then turned to hoovering up the floating bits. Having now freed the rope, I hauled in the slack until I had possession of the remaining three crays. Then I turned around and swam as fast as my flippers would take me across the reef to the boat. I dived over the gunwale, pulling my catch after me, and decided that three crays were enough for one day.

The Saga of the DC3

The local Bialla airstrip was a fairly short runway cut out of the coconut plantations. It ran from the beach into the bush. You could only land and take off in one direction, which meant approaching from the seaward end and taking off from the inland end. There was a four-metre drop from the end of the airstrip down to the water, and this drop was often utilised by aircraft to help them become airborne if there was no on-shore breeze to assist take-off—particularly if they were heavily laden.

The only commercial aircraft that used that strip were STOL (short take-off and landing) types, such as the turbo-propped Twin Otter with its large wing span, and the single engine, turbo prop, tail-wheel Pilatus Porter. The other aircraft that used the strip were small, single engine Cessna 185, 177, 172, and Auster aircraft, mainly owned by the Missionary Aviation Fellowship (MAF). MAF aircraft were used to service the missions and some remote villages and were flown by young Aussie and Kiwi pilots aiming to get their commercial hours up so that they could apply for a job with a commercial airline.

One of the commercial airlines based at Rabaul owned an ex-Trans Australia Airlines (TAA) DC3 *balus* (plane), which was used for passengers and freight from Rabaul to the longer airstrips such as Open Bay, Talasea, Sag Sag, Jaquinot Bay, and Kavieng. The pilot who flew the DC3 was suddenly transferred to the PNG mainland, and the airline had to quickly find a replacement. The young Aussie replacement pilot arrived later than scheduled and only had time to do one quick round of the DC3-capable airstrips before he was let loose on his own.

He took off from Rabaul on his first pilot-in-command flight, lightly loaded (fortunately), and headed down the coast. The first stop was Sule (originally called Ubili), located between Ulamona and Open Bay, which he found without any problem and duly landed. He off-loaded some cargo, took on a couple of passengers, and took off again heading for Talasea. Unfortunately for him, there were numerous bays and half a dozen airstrips scattered along the coast, and they all came in directly off the sea at 90 degrees to the coastline, ending up in the coconut plantations. From the air, and from the viewpoint of a pilot who had only flown the route once before as a passenger, most of these airstrips looked the same.

The young pilot spotted a likely looking contender for the Talasea strip, lined up, and brought the old plane in over the beach. He put her down nicely only a few metres in from the drop off, then feathered the props and applied the brakes. About half-way up the runway he thought, "Bugger, this strip looks a bit short!" He tried valiantly to push his feet through the floor as he put maximum pressure on the brakes, but with limited results. With the wheels locked up, the old plane skidded the last 40 metres and slid into the swamp at the end of the runway, where it stopped dead. Welcome to Bialla airstrip!

There was no-one about on the Bialla strip to witness the event except one old *meri* who had been minding her own business and working in her garden off to one side of the airstrip. There was no-one to meet the aircraft because there were no flights scheduled for that day. By this time, the pilot had woken up to his mistake and realised that he must have landed on the wrong airstrip, so he frantically radioed the Rabaul control tower to apprise them of his dilemma. Soon the entire local population, having heard the sound of an unscheduled *balus* landing, arrived in force and stood around offering "expert" advice—none of it particularly practical.

The company that owned the DC3 sent down a Twin Otter later that day to take off the passengers, and the next day the company flew in the aviation experts. A few days later, engineers were flown in. They borrowed the *Kiap's* tractor and one of Farid's log skidders, tied ropes around the plane's tail-wheel, and towed the DC3 backwards out of the swamp. The plane was undamaged, as it had almost stopped by the time it ran into the swamp.

So the plane was out of the swamp, but now the engineers needed to get it out of Bialla. They started up the engines and motored over to the side of the strip next to the tin shed that masqueraded as the Bialla terminal, where they proceeded to strip everything possible out of the plane; seats, cabin linings, toilet, bulkheads—anything that could be removed was removed. To make the plane lighter still, the engineers drained the fuel so that there was only enough to allow the plane to take off and fly the short distance down the coast to Talasea, the nearest DC3 capable airstrip.

The next move was to bring in an experienced DC3 pilot from Port Moresby to recover the aircraft. When he arrived at Bialla, he checked the plane over, then motored the old girl back up to the end of the airstrip and swung her around with the tail-wheel about a 30 centimetres short of the swamp. The engineers attached a custom-made quick-release clamp arrangement to the tail-wheel assembly. All four of us resident expats were now involved in the rescue effort. We drove the log skidder into the swamp and then winched the *Kiap's* tractor in after it, creating an anchor for the plane. Then we tied one end of a couple of heavy duty nylon ropes to the skidder, looped the ropes through the quick-release clamp on the plane's tail-wheel, then tied the other end to the *Kiap's* tractor.

The take-off attempt was timed for very early in the morning when there was a light breeze blowing in off the sea. The on-shore breeze coupled with cooler early morning temperatures were critical to assist in giving the plane more power and lift when she took off. One engineer stood by for the pilot's signal, and another crouched on the ground by the tail-wheel, making sure that he was forward of the rope and well clear of the bight. The pilot wound the DC3 up to full revs until she was fair howling, and when he gave the signal that he was ready to roll, the standing engineer gave the signal to the tail-wheel engineer. He yanked back on the quick-release lever, and the rope and clamp sprang back into the swamp with such force that they would have cut in half anyone who had been standing in the way!

The plane shot forward and barrelled down the strip, while the assembled throng held our collective breath. The tail-wheel lifted off, but the DC3 was still in front wheel contact with the ground when she reached the end of the runway. The plane dropped at least a metre over the four-metre high bank to the beach, and everyone gasped, but at the same time the old DC3 became airborne! She appeared to be skimming just across the surface of the water, and then at last she gained a bit of height, lifted up, and flew away. Boy, that was close!

The DC3 arrived safely in Talasea. Had the plane not been completely stripped out, she certainly wouldn't have made it off the runway, let alone to her intended destination.

The company then brought a Twin Otter into Bialla to shuttle all the stripped-out fittings back to Rabaul, where the DC3 was eventually re-assembled. The whole process had taken nearly three weeks, and the airline was once again looking for a new pilot to fly their plane.

Barge of Corpses

I had been working up the coast and was just preparing to leave the last logging operation of the day to head home, when a Toyota pick-up came screaming down to the beach in a cloud of dust. The driver shouted out that a serious accident had just occurred up in the bush, and I was requested to report it to the *Kiap* at Ewasse.

Apparently, a fully loaded Nissan logging truck had been heading down to the beach with four Sepik loggers sitting on the bull-bars on the front of the truck, together with their chainsaws and all of their gear. While coming down a particularly steep hill, the truck's radiator hose had burst firing boiling water through the radiator grill and all over the riders on the bull-bar. In the resulting panic, the loggers had either jumped or fallen from the bull-bars and been run over by the truck. All four had been killed.

I headed on back to Ewasse and notified the *Kiap*. He radioed the Rabaul police to report the incident and arrange for a plane to pick the bodies up at the Bialla airstrip, from where they could be flown back to their home villages in the south of Papua for burial, as was the custom.

The next day the four bodies, wrapped in sheets, were taken down to the beach and loaded onto a small, flat-topped cargo barge and towed to Bialla. The barge reached the Bialla airstrip just after midday, but there was no sign of any plane. Apparently, Rabaul was having trouble finding a plane that wasn't committed to a regular commercial service, but they sent a message to say that they would keep trying.

At about five p.m., with no plane in evidence, the boat and its barge turned around and headed back up the coast to the logging camp. The local natives at Nantabu had insisted that the barge return back to the camp with the corpses, because local customs didn't allow foreign bodies to hang around in their territory—it was felt that the spirits of the Sepiks would clash with their own local spirits and cause all sorts of problems.

The next morning, the barge turned up again off the Bialla airstrip with its macabre cargo and waited in vain for a plane that never came. That evening, boat and barge returned to the beach off their logging camp once again. On the third day, the same performance was repeated, but due to the intense tropical heat and the fact that the corpses had been lying for three days and nights out on the open steel-topped barge, they were now seriously rank, and we could smell them coming up the coast from a mile away. The crew operating the tow-boat had wet towels wrapped around their faces to try to mask the smell.

On the fourth day, the barge again arrived off the Bialla airstrip, and fortunately, around 11 a.m., so did a single-engine Cessna 185. The bodies were wrapped up in additional fresh sheets, carried from the barge to the beach, and loaded onto the plane.

The young Aussie pilot who had been chartered out of Lae on the mainland hadn't been flying for very long in PNG, and this was his first corpse delivery. Unfortunately for him, these particular bodies were putrid to beat the band! I felt sorry for the poor bugger. He took off with his head sticking out of the side window, and he told me when I met him again a couple of months later, that he flew with his nose out of the window for the entire trip to the Sepik. It was a journey of some 800 kilometres, so he had to put down at Lae en-route in order to refuel. The corpses were so putrid, the pilot reckoned, that it had taken weeks to get the stink out of the plane, and he had had to burn his clothes when he got back to Lae.

Trouble in Paradise

The local natives in the Ewasse area were good people; generally friendly, like most people from the coastal tribes. I never really encountered any dodgy moments except for the one time. I had been working up in the jungle on the far northern boundary of the Pacific Logging concession and was heading home on my motor bike. For some reason, I had decided to take a shortcut home through the network of village walking tracks. As I approached Buso, the second to last village before Ewasse, I slowed down in expectation of the *pikininis* and dogs that were usually playing or lying on any track near a village. Other than a couple of barking dogs, which I swerved to avoid, it seemed to be all clear. But just before I passed the last group of houses, a little *pikinini meri* ran out onto the track, cannoned into my boot and promptly sat down with a bump in the middle of the track. She wasn't injured at all but had got quite a fright and started crying her head off.

I stopped to make sure that the *pikinini* was all right, and I picked her up and dusted her off. She was still crying when about a dozen villagers ran out from their houses, spotted the white man with the motorbike and the little girl crying, and immediately assumed that I had hit and injured her. The white man was always to blame in these circumstances. The cry went up: "*Kilem em, kilem em!*" ("Kill him!"), and more villagers ran out waving machetes.

I thought, "Bugger, I might be in a spot of bother here."

I tried reasoning with them and explained that the *pikinini* had run out from behind a bush on the edge of the track and bumped into me before I could stop. I assured them that she wasn't really injured, just frightened. They were in no mood to be reasoned with, however, and things were looking decidedly dicey.

I was trying to figure out how to get out of this situation in one piece when one of my native Forestry Assistants heard the commotion and came to investigate. He lived in that village and had just arrived home from work. He quickly assessed the situation and shouted to the mob to back off. He told them that this was *Masta* Ross, that I was the District Forest Officer from Ewasse and his boss, and that I was one of the good guys.

Fortunately, he must have been sufficiently well respected in the village, as he was able to calm the volatile situation and let me explain what had happened. He picked the *pikinini meri* up, who by this time had stopped crying, showed them that she was not injured, and they eventually settled down. I jumped back onto my bike and rode off while the going was good. That was a bit of a close call and the only potentially bad situation that I encountered with these locals.

I did, however, manage to scare myself one day when I was way out in the jungle surveying a new block of forest for Pacific Lumber. I had a day-pack with my lunch and survey gear in it and was wearing my jungle boots. I came to a river that had to be crossed, but which had very steep banks. After walking up and down the bank for a bit, trying unsuccessfully to find a place to get down to the water, I eventually came to a 3 metre high bank above a bend in the river where the water looked to be only about a metre deep against the bank and the bottom sloped gradually up to a shingle beach on the other side . This appeared to be the only suitable place that I could get down, so I jumped off the bank into the river.

Unfortunately for me, the depth of the crystal-clear water was deceptive, and it was more like two and a half or three metres deep. I went straight to the bottom, with my head well below the surface. There was a fair sort of current running on the bend, and I was heavy in the water with my pack now saturated. I was still holding on to my machete, and my boots were full of water, which weighed me down. Even though I tried and tried, I couldn't kick my way back up to the surface.

I hadn't taken a deep breath before jumping in because I had thought that the water was only up to my chest, so now I started to get a bit worried. As I was being swept down-stream with the current, I ran along the bottom, desperately trying to stay upright, while trying to reach the other side where the riverbed sloped up to the gravel beach. I was seriously short of oxygen, but I kept on running and trying to work my way across to the other side.

Eventually, I managed to make some headway, edging closer and closer to the far side of the river. At last I felt the bottom start to slope upwards under my feet! By this time, I had run out of oxygen and was very near drowning. Then I felt the top of my head break the surface.

The water was still too deep to get my head clear, but this gave me the impetus to bend my knees and make an upwards lunge with my last remaining energy. On the third jump, I managed to get my mouth above the water for a fraction of a second, which was enough to gulp in some of that sweet fresh air before I sank back down again. That brief gulp of air enabled me to make those last few steps to climb up the loose, sloping gravel bed and get my head out of the water. I finally crawled out of the river on my hands and knees, totally knackered, and lay flat out on the river bank for about a quarter of an hour before I regained enough strength to get back on my feet and start walking again. Just another blip on the learning curve in the life of a Forest Ranger!

The politics of the international log markets at that time were out there in cowboy territory and brought their own kind of trouble. I had been at Ewasse for about six months when my counterpart DFO, who was responsible for half a dozen logging operations on the same coast but north-east of my territory, went off on extended sick leave. I was asked to look after his three southern-most operations along with mine. The northern-most three would be looked after by someone from the Rabaul office. The additional operations that I was allocated were Baia (where the DFO's house was), Lolobau Island, and Ulamona. Getting to these operations meant a fair hike up the coast for me, but I could do all three in one day if I left very early in the morning—and so long as the wind didn't get up, I could make it home just on dark.

Tucked away to the far east of Open Bay was a small secluded bay sheltered by an island which was practically connected to the mainland, called Kakolan Island. This bay was being used as the log holding pond of the Weyerhaeuser Company. Weyerhaeuser is a big American forestry and logging company. At that time, it had operations in the Philippines and Indonesia, with log markets in Japan, Korea, and Europe. Their log buyer at that time was a Kiwi forester by the name of Warren Travers, and he had been buying selected logs from the small private operators along the coast and rafting them to a holding pond deep inside Kakolan Bay.

At that time, Japan was the primary market for mixed tropical New Guinea hardwoods. The Japanese had this cunning scheme: whenever the log prices crept up a bit too high for their liking, they declared that the Japanese log ports were full. They would then stop buying and put a hold on all log shipments until they decided that it was time to buy again. Of course, this was just a ploy to drive the log prices down, as they knew that all their suppliers' holding stocks would deteriorate if they weren't shipped within a couple of months following production.

Most of the smaller suppliers just sold their stocks immediately and accepted whatever price the Japs were offering, because they couldn't afford to hold onto the logs. The prices they were forced to accept in this situation, however, were often below the production costs. Warren, decided to hold onto his Open Bay stocks because Weyerhaeuser also had log production out of the Phillipines and Indonesia to consider, so they couldn't afford to bow too low to the Japanese.

Consequently, when I arrived at the bay beside Kakolan Island in late 1972, I found some 9,000-odd tonnes of once beautiful New Guinea hardwood logs sitting on the bottom of the holding pond, waterlogged, full of teredo worms, and worthless. What a waste! But that was the way of the tropical hardwood log markets in those days.

Weyerhaeuser wasn't the only company to lose to Japanese log market price manipulation. In mid-1972, the always potentially-fragile Shin Asahigawa-Lebanese-Pacific

Lumber marriage at Bialla suffered a messy divorce, mainly due to the Japanese side of the arrangement reneging on their agreed minimum log price to the Lebanese operators. The usual Japanese trick of holding back ships to screw the log prices down to below production cost didn't work with Farid. He just dug in his toes and shut down his logging operations. When the Japanese partners chartered a plane in Rabaul and flew in a delegation to demand that he re-start logging and deliver the logs to the wharf, regardless of the price that they were paying, Farid, waving his loaded shotgun, jumped into his Jeep, and—screaming at them alternatively in Lebanese, English and Pidgin—chased them all the way back to the Bialla airport, where they hastily jumped back into their chartered plane and flew away, never to be seen again!

More threatening than a wild and angry Lebanese logger however, were the weather and the sea, and I had my fair share of close encounters with these over my time in PNG. One such encounter I shall never forget.

I needed some more building materials from the government stores at Cape Hoskins, so I used the *Kiap's* radio telephone and contacted the Forestry Department office in Kimbe to ask if they could help me. When I first arrived in Rabaul, I had been told that the DFO in Hoskins was another Kiwi by the name of Bill Robinson. I had never heard of a Bill Robinson in New Zealand, so I assumed that he must be from a Ranger School intake prior to ours. The radio operator in Hoskins finally got hold of Bill Robinson and connected him up with Ewasse radio.

I said, "Hullo, is that Bill Robinson? This is Ross Lockyer here, from Ewasse."

The voice on the other end sounded familiar— especially when it shouted: "Bloody hell, Lockyer! What are you doing there?"

I nearly dropped the radio mic. I said, "Is that you, Herb?"

Yep, it sure was! It was my old mate, Herb Robinson, also known as Mark Robinson (but never Bill), from our 1962 Ranger School intake. I had last seen Herb in November 1964 (eight years previously), when we completed our Rotorua Ranger School year. Herb had been a New Zealand Forest Products ranger trainee. He had returned to Tokoroa in January 1965 but had left for elsewhere by the time I arrived there in mid-1966.

Anyway, we had a good yarn, I ordered my supplies, and we arranged that I would take my boat down to Hoskins one weekend when the sea was flat enough and have a proper catch-up. Some weeks later, I did make the trip and enjoyed a very pleasant weekend and quite a few SPs with Herb and his wife, Carmel.

The homeward trip on the Sunday afternoon, however, was a bit of a mission. During my stay in Hoskins, I had met an Aussie girl called Yolanda who lived and worked at a mission station back up the coast, about halfway between Hoskins and Ewasse near the village of Tarobi. She had been visiting friends at another mission station at Hoskins and was looking for a way to get back home. I told her that she was welcome to travel with me and that I would drop her off at Tarobi on my way home.

Once around Cape Hoskins heading east, however, our route took us across the wide and open Commodore Bay. Commodore Bay was well known for chopping up quite badly in the afternoons, so we left at about 10 a.m. from Hoskins to try to cross the Bay before the wind got up. We had only travelled a few kilometres when a sudden squall came up from the north; it was packing quite a strong wind with horizontal rain. The sea in the Bay quickly chopped up to quite a nasty state, but we were too far from Cape Hoskins to turn back, and visibility had become very poor in the rain.

I kept tacking in and out of the chop to retain some semblance of stability. My little 14-footer was quite narrow-gutted and not the greatest sea boat in bad weather. She rolled and pitched a lot, and took on a fair amount of water. I instructed my now rather frightened passenger to grab the bailer, which was half a coconut shell, and start bailing as fast as she could. The bailing at least kept her mind off the choppy sea and the lack of visibility. I was concerned that we were getting too far out into the Bay, and I was fast losing sight of land in the heavy rain.

I swung the boat northwards, towards the coast, but now the swell was coming right under the stern. I figured that if we were going to have to swim for it, then the closer I could get to land the better. Of course, I didn't have any of that superfluous stuff like life jackets, radio, flares, compass, or anything, but Peter had told me when I bought the boat that it had flotation built into the seats and under the foredeck and wasn't supposed to sink even if it filled with water. I just hoped that he was right! After about an hour of battling the chop, and with Yolanda keeping us afloat with the bailer, the squall disappeared as quickly as it had arrived.

The rain stopped, the wind dropped, and the chop started to ease off.

Once I had reasonable visibility again and could run across the chop, I was able to swing the boat back onto an eastern heading and head once again to Bakoba Point and Tarobi. We arrived at Tarobi a couple of hours later than we had planned, totally saturated, but at least in one piece. Yolanda was quite a cute chick and one of the very few single expatriate girls to be found anywhere between Rabaul and Cape Hoskins. However, my hopes for a possible future date were somewhat dampened when she told me unequivocally that there was no way that she would get into a boat as small, wet, and unstable as mine again. I was welcome, however, to come and visit her at the mission station where she worked.

I had stayed at plenty of mission stations around PNG over the years, and I was fully aware of the limitations that would be placed on my activities while visiting a pretty girl who was living there. My style would be cramped more than somewhat, so I fuzzed it and told her that I would try to get down again if I ever had the opportunity—but of course I never did.

So, I dropped her off at the mission jetty and headed back home to Ewasse.

The Legend of Fred Hargesheimer

At Nantabu village near Ewasse there was a school, and beside the school was a simple but comfortable, tropical style house. There was no-one living in the house when I first arrived, but after about a month the owners flew in and took up residence. That house belonged to a couple of the most interesting people that I ever had the pleasure to meet; they were Fred and Dorothy Hargesheimer. I soon got to know them very well. I often had dinner at their place, and we had long discussions into the night, mostly about our mutual interest in PNG cultures and ethnology. I would drop fresh fish in to them regularly, as I almost always caught far more than we could eat at the government station.

Sitting in Fred and Dorothy's sitting room after dinner, we would yarn far into the night. Over many evenings, I gradually squeezed the most fascinating story out of them about how this couple ended up living in this remotest of remote locations.

Fred was an extremely modest man and was reluctant to admit that he had achieved anything particularly special in his life, but the reality was very different.

Fred had been an American army pilot during World War II, and in 1943 he had been shot down by the Japanese over West New Britain. He was lucky to have parachuted out of his crippled P-38 reconnaissance plane before it crashed into the jungle.

Fred survived for a month in the deep jungle until he was found by local hunters from the Nakanai tribe. He was in very poor condition when the Nakanais found him, and he was suffering from various illnesses as well as from malnutrition. The hunters took him back to their village near the coast and nursed him back to health, while all the time hiding him from the Japanese patrols. Some eight months after he had been shot down, he was contacted by Australian commandos who were working behind the Japanese lines, and he was eventually picked up off a beach near Ewasse by an American submarine.

When Fred retired in 1960, he flew back to New Britain and revisited the village of Ea Ea near Ewasse where he had spent part of his recovery time during the war. He saw that the village was still very poor, but what they needed more than anything was education for the children as well as medical assistance. Fred went back to the States, raised the money, and returned 3 years later to build a school at Ea Ea village. Over the next 10 years he raised more money and built a medical clinic and more schools at Ea Ea (later renamed Nantabu) and the surrounding Nakanai villages.

In 1970, Fred and Dorothy moved to Nantabu, built the house where they were now living, and the pair of them were actually teaching at the Nantabu village school when I was there. Fred was also developing an experimental oil palm nursery and plantation for the benefit of the schools and the local villagers, and he was very proud to show me the beginnings of what soon developed into a thriving and viable industry in that area.

Fred often told me that if it wasn't for the Nakanai hunters finding him, and the people looking after him and protecting him, then he wouldn't be there now. He was very grateful that he was able to spend his retirement years trying to repay them for what they had done for him.

I read recently that Fred died back in the States in 2010 at the ripe old age of 94.

Fred was a fine human being, and a man whom I was very proud to have known.

The Amazing Machinery of Father *Buai*

On the West New Britain coast just south of Lolobau Island is the village of Ulamona, which I always enjoyed visiting, as it had a very interesting timber operation.

It was only a small logging operation with one D7 bulldozer, an old truck, and a log loader. At Ulamona, however, there was no log export. The Ulamona operation had an amazing sawmill that was used to convert all of its log production into sawn timber for sale up and down the New Britain coast and even as far as the New Guinea mainland.

Although the first colonial government in Papua was established in 1884, the first forestry activity was not initiated until 1908 when an Australian forester made a brief appraisal of the timber resource. A timber ordinance came into effect in 1909 in both territories—Papua and New Guinea, and the first commercial sawmill in the country began operations at Ulamona, West New Britain Province, in 1898.

The mill and the logging operation at Ulamona was (and still is) owned by the Capuchin Catholic Mission, and the man that managed everything during my days in the region was an old German priest known only as Father *Buai* (pronounced "boo-eye").

Buai is the Pidgin word for betel nut, which commonly used all over PNG and South East Asia. The green betel nut (*buai*) is first put in the mouth and chewed, then a bit of lime powder (*kambang*), and mustard (*daka*—a bean-like green vegetable) is added into the mouth, and then everything is chewed together. The first thing you notice in PNG is that almost all the native men and women have brilliant, red-stained teeth and lips, and that they spit red betel juice all over the place.

Father *Buai* was a habitual *buai* chewer from way back, hence his nick-name. He always had quid of *buai* working away in his cheek. No-one that I ever spoke to knew what his real name was, as he had always been known to natives and expatriates alike as Father Buai. He had been at Ulamona seemingly forever—since the Germans ran the country before the Second World War. What happened to him during the war was never made clear, but it is probable that he hid in the jungle with the natives until the Japs were finally chased out. Or he may have just stayed put, as the Germans and Japanese were good mates at the time.

The Ulamona sawmill was a work of art. The entire mill was run off an old British steam engine that gleamed and shone through constant polishing and care. The old steam engine drove a series of shafts and overhead pulleys with big wide belts running down from the ceiling to the pulleys that drove the saws. Everything was so finely adjusted, greased, oiled, and aligned that you could stand in the middle of the mill with the steam engine running and every saw spinning at full speed, and—provided there was no timber being sawn at the time—you could hear someone speaking in a normal voice 10 metres away. In fact, it was a little eerie and quite surreal.

The native sawyers had been working there all their lives, as had their fathers before them. Father *Buai* was an amazing old guy who spoke only Pidgin and the local native dialect, and he treated all the workers like his children.

The mill itself was only part of it though. Between the mill and the beach was a big timber yard with all the sawn timber stacked by species and size, ready for sale. The sawmill floor, which was all made of hardwood, was dead flat, and the hardwood deck continued out through the front of the mill and through the yard to the top of the beach. It was all perfectly level and stable at every point.

The Ulamona mill was supplied with logs from the jungle concession by means of a heavy steel tramline, while a light tramline carried wood from the mill to the storage yard and thence to the jetty. All through the mill and adjacent to each saw—running out of the mill, through the yard, and out to the beach—were narrow gauge tramline rails. These were embedded so that the tops were flush with the floor. The timber was stacked onto wooden trolleys as it came off the saws and then, with one man pushing a loaded trolley with very little effort, it rolled out of the mill, around the corners, and was stopped alongside the correct timber stack where it was then unloaded. The timber decking and the rails were so perfectly level at every part of the mill and yard that one man could push a trolley with over a tonne of timber anywhere around the mill and yard on his own and with minimal effort!

The sawn timber that was produced at Ulamona was known all over New Britain and beyond as the most perfectly dimensioned sawn timber in the country. Every Ulamona-made board was perfect in size and gauge. If you wanted the best sawn timber in all of PNG, you bought it from Father *Buai* at Ulamona.

I always enjoyed my visits to Ulamona and lunch with Father *Buai*. He was a great character and story-teller, and I never tired of listening to him and watching that beautiful old steam engine at work.

Remotest of the Remote

In late 1972, I was transferred to Mendi in the Southern Highlands of PNG. The resident District Forest Officer, Phil Waring, was returning to New Zealand, and a replacement was urgently needed. The Southern Highlands was new territory for me, as I had previously only ventured up as far as Mt Hagen in the Western Highlands.

The Southern Highlands is PNG's most remote and most recently discovered territory. Its hidden mountain valleys and towering limestone peaks were, in fact, only discovered by Europeans as late as 1935. The territory contains PNG's second highest mountain, Mt Giluwe (4,368 metres), and the climate is cool and comfortable. Margarima, one of the outstations that I frequently visited high in the mountains, became very cold after about 4 p.m., and a thick jersey or jacket was always required in case one had to spend the night.

The Southern Highlands is home to the Huli people, and the men are renowned for the large and elaborate, human hair wigs that they wear. These wigs are generally decorated with everlasting daisies, and the Huli men usually paint their faces brightly with yellow and ochre. Both men and women wear traditional dress at all times, even when tending their gardens and pigs, or building their huts.

Sorcery and witchcraft are an integral part of everyday life throughout most of Papua New Guinea even to this day, but nowhere is sorcery more entrenched than in the Highlands. When I lived in the Southern Highlands in 1972–73, torture and killing of "witches" was a common occurrence throughout the region, and there are terrible "witch" killings and torture of so-called witches frequently reported to this present day. Alleged witches—mostly women, but some men and even children, are subjected to horrific torture before being hanged, burned alive, or thrown off cliffs.

PNG was an Australian controlled territory when I lived there, and the *Kiaps* and their native auxiliaries attempted to suppress sorcery killings to some extent, at least within their patrol territories. Since independence, however, the old ways have undergone a gruesome renaissance—and nowhere more so than in the Highlands.

Back in 1972, Mendi, the capital of the Southern Highlands, was in the middle of the most remote area of PNG and at the end of the Highlands Highway, although that Highway now extends a further 227 kilometres to Lake Kopiago. It was a government town with a resident Provincial High Commissioner, all the Provincial Government offices and the busy Mendi airport. There were numerous traders, coffee buyers, Local Government officers, and local airline pilots. The airport was an important part of the service and supply industry at Mendi, as most of the outstations could only be accessed by air.

I had thirteen forestry outstations in my territory, but I could only drive to one of them—Ialibu. Even the Mendi-Ialibu road required a four-wheel drive vehicle, and the road was often impassable in the rainy season.

Between June and October 1972, a series of severe frosts destroyed almost all the subsistence food gardens above 2,000 metres in the Western and Southern Highlands. The upper Lai and Marient valleys in the Kandep basin, the

Margarima area, and the upper Mendi and Kaugel valleys were the worst affected areas. In early October, more frosts occurred in areas as low as 1,600 metres that previously had not been affected, including the Ialibu basin, localities near Kagua, Nipa, Poroma, Tari, Wabag, Wapenamanda, and parts of the Wahgi valley. Altogether, the gardens and many of the surrounding tree shelter belts belonging to some 150,000 people were badly damaged, and there was a consequent severe shortage of food.

Because of the threat of famine, a State of Emergency was declared in October, and a major relief operation was undertaken. Aid was given in the form of rice, tinned meat and fish, sweet potato runners, Irish potatoes, and vegetable seeds. These were flown into Mendi in RAAF Hercules aircraft and further distributed to nearby villages by road where possible, and by light aircraft and helicopters to the more remote locations. Due to the fact that *kaukau* (sweet potato), the staple diet of the native New Guinean, takes nine months to mature, aid was continued for over six months.

I arrived right in the middle of all this, and a big part of my new responsibilities was to set up new (and upgrade existing) outstation tree nurseries in the frost-affected areas. The role of these nurseries was to propagate, supply, and plant seedlings for the replacement and establishment of mainly *Pandanus, Ficus,* and *Casuarina* trees for shelter belts around the new gardens to protect them from future frosts. The value of shelter belts was well proven: many of the gardens with established shelter belts had not been totally wiped out by the frosts.

I arrived at my new office to find that the role of DFO Southern Highlands Region was considered important enough to require its own secretary! She was an Aussie girl named Marion who had a young son, and she lived in a house up on the hill behind my own *donga* in the town. As Phil had to depart only two days after my arrival, Marion was invaluable in assisting me to become familiar with the territory, the outstations, my native staff, and "who was who in the zoo" in Mendi.

I was on the phone one day to Goroka in the Eastern Highlands to discuss the transfer of a couple of native Forest Rangers from Goroka to Mendi. After I had talked to the senior native ranger, he put me onto his boss, the DFO for the Eastern Highlands. That old familiar voice came on the line, and lo and behold if it wasn't Herb Robinson again! He had been transferred to the Eastern Highlands not long after I had arrived in the Southern Highlands. We had a catch-up once more, but that was the last time I talked to Herb until some 40 years later, when we met in Reefton on the West Coast of New Zealand's South Island at the 50th Forest Ranger School Reunion. Herb was then living in Cairns, Australia.

The main forestry outstations that had already been established and some of those that I needed to upgrade were located at Lake Kopiago and Koroba in the far north-west of the province, Tari and Nipa to the east, Margarima (located at 2,556 metres, high in the mountains), Erave and Poroma to the south, and Ialibu, Kagua, and Pangia to the east.

The nature of my territory meant that my transport arrangements were rather complex. I was supplied with a Yamaha 150cc motor cycle for transport around Mendi, from home to office, and to the airstrip. To get to Ialibu, when the road was open, I could hitch a ride with any one of a number of other government officers in a four-wheel drive Land Cruiser from the government motor pool. To get me to everywhere else (which was 95 percent of my travel), Marion would phone the government transport office the day before and book me a seat on a Macair or Talair plane to wherever it was that I was going.

Because I was travelling regularly to all my outstations, which were in some of the most remote locations in the Southern Highlands, I was often the only passenger— although sometimes we would pick up a *Kiap*, or a *Didiman*, or one of the emergency aid officers from another location either en-route or on the way home. The pilot would normally drop me off in the morning at my destination and pick me up again later in the afternoon. Due to the frequently unpredictable weather in the Highlands, however, the pickup was often postponed until the next day.

There were usually five or six aircraft stationed permanently at Mendi, although this increased to more than a dozen during the State of Emergency aid period. They were a mixture of makes, models and capabilities, because the airstrips in the Southern Highlands varied in length, altitude, and surface condition. Only the Mendi strip was long and sealed, while most of the others were relatively short, and surfaced with grass or packed clay. The permanent single-engine aircraft included a tail-wheel Cessna 185, a couple of Cessna 206's that were faster and more comfortable than the 185 but which needed a longer strip, and a smaller Cessna 172 that could handle short airstrips but only had seating for the pilot and three passengers. Then there were two faster and more comfortable twin engine aircraft that needed longer airstrips than the single engine planes. These were a

Beechcraft Baron and a Piper Aztec. Which aircraft I used depended on where I was going, how many other passengers or how much cargo were booked, and which aircraft was available on the day.

The furthest and most remote outstation that I had to fly to regularly was Tari. Lake Kopiago was further west, but as that area hadn't been so affected by the frost I didn't go there so often. The route from Mendi to Tari passed through numerous high mountain passes and around many sharp peaks that were often covered in cloud caps. The cloud could come in fast and unpredictably in those high mountains. The Tari flight was always risky, and the pilots had to watch the weather constantly and be prepared to turn back or take evasive action at any time, especially in the afternoons when the weather became more unpredictable. Because of the altitude at which we had to fly, the possibility that we might have to dive out of a pass in a hurry to avoid a clag-in, the unpredictable weather, and the preference for two engines for safety reasons, we usually flew the Tari route in either the Baron or the Aztec. The Tari airstrip was built extra-long to accommodate these twin-engine planes.

I knew all the pilots based at Mendi. They were young Aussies and Kiwis who were flying over what was the most dangerous flying terrain in the country, and they were working there because they needed to clock up their commercial flying hours. This would enable them to apply for the higher-paying jobs flying larger commercial aircraft for the recognised airlines.

The only other way to clock up hours was to fly the small Cessna 177, 172, or 170 planes for MAF (Missionary Aviation Fellowship), which was a last resort for some, but in many cases the only option. Most of the Mendi pilots had flown previously for MAF before landing jobs with the small charter airlines such as Macair and Talair. MAF only paid pocket money and provided bed and board, usually at a mission station. The remote mission station airstrips were short, precarious, and often downright dangerous. We used to fly over some of them en-route to Tari or Margarima, and I couldn't believe that any sane pilot would land on them. There was one that was nothing more than a narrow ledge, hand-cut out of the side of a mountain, with a cliff face at one end. If you landed down the centre of that strip in a small tail-wheel Cessna (and you could only land in one direction), then your port wing tip would be no more than 15-20 metres from the cliff face, and the starboard wing tip would be hanging out into space over a shear drop of 200 or more metres to the valley below. The plane had to be turned around manually by the villagers at the far end of the strip so it could take off in the opposite direction to that in which it had landed. Little wonder that the MAF pilots had been nick-named "the kamikaze boys". Crashes and fatalities in light planes were all too frequent in PNG, especially in the Highlands.

Surviving the Tari Gap

Then there was the infamous "Tari Gap"—the monster in the mountains. It was known and feared by pilots and travellers alike and was the cause of many plane crashes and fatalities over the years. Mendi town was located at 1,855 metres above sea level, and the only route through the mountains to Tari, which lay at 2,167 metres above sea-level, was through the Tari Gap.

After zig-zagging through the mountains and gaining height wherever possible, we had to fly through the Gap, the gut or base of which is about 2,750 metres. So, we first had to gain about 1,000 metres in altitude from Mendi. The Gap itself is about 1.5 kilometres wide at the top between the peaks, but when the cloud drops, then the passage through the Gap becomes very narrow. It appeared not to be much wider than the aircraft when we were close in on approach. Once through, we had to immediately drop about 700 metres to the Tari Airfield which was almost vertically below us. That wasn't even the tricky bit.

The Tari Gap is a narrow pass between two peaks, which are each about 3,350 metres high—some 600 metres above the base of the Gap. Under good weather conditions the cloud base hangs around the tops of the peaks in the morning, so once we located the Gap, there was usually good clear air in and above the Gap allowing the plane to fly safely through. The first time through the Gap was a bit of a hair-raiser if the cloud ceiling was down though, because the hard bits on either side of the plane seemed so close that you felt you could reach out and touch them.

The southern end of the Tari airstrip ends about six metres above a swampy depression filled with tall cane grass. On the other side of the swamp, about 900 metres away, is the Kupari Catholic Mission station. As a plane took off from Tari it would wallow out over the cane grass on what initially appeared to be a short but fatal flight into a row of tall klinkii pines surrounding the priest's house. In one of those ironic twists of colonial history, the mission, having cut down all the pines on nearby *Huli* sacred sites in order to mill them and build the church, had replanted the same tree species around their own sacred site!

The approach to the Tari Saddle itself is covered in *kunai* grass and low scrub, and on either side loom the two massive forest-covered volcanoes, Ambua and Gerowa, both over 3,350 metres in height. On the southern side, the saddle rolls gently down into the Margarima River valley, while on the northern side it drops sharply into the Tari Basin.

The most challenging part of flying through the Tari Gap was going home in the afternoon. I can recall standing on the Tari airstrip at about 3 p.m., waiting for a plane to return to pick me up. Looking straight up above me at the mountains I could see the Gap some 600 metres directly above me, and there was still some clear air between the Gap and the peaks. Then I would spot the plane shooting through the hole like a cork popping out of a bottle, and diving and cork-screwing down to the airfield. I clambered aboard with the engines still running, and we immediately took off and started the long, slow climb back up to the Gap.

As we flew around and around to gain altitude, looking up we could see the cloud base dropping fast off the high peaks, and the clear hole through the Gap rapidly getting smaller. The question was, as always: "Are we going to make it in time?" We silently urged the plane to climb faster, but the cloud was dropping quicker than we were climbing. We finally got up to 2,780 metres, put the nose down and headed straight in toward the Gap, with the throttles wide open. The cloud base, by this time, was barely 30 metres above the floor of the Gap, and dropping fast.

This was the point of decision. Now we were flying straight and level and aiming for the Gap at a point about 40 metres above the deck. Even though the cloud was rapidly shutting the Gap down, we only needed sufficient visibility to hold the aircraft on course and altitude. Then we could shoot through the closing cloud where we had last spotted the Gap, and we would be home and hosed. Once through the hole, we nosed down immediately out of the cloud, veering slightly to the left and navigating around the mountains and through the passes until we worked our way back to Mendi.

That time we made it, but sometimes the cloud beat us to it and there was no Gap to fly through by the time we had gained sufficient altitude to negotiate it. In such cases, we just had to turn around and spiral back down to Tari.

On all flights to Tari I took an overnight bag so that, when I couldn't make it out, I could check into the government guest house for the night. It was very basic accommodation, but at least it provided a bed and a feed. The pilot and I would head off again early the next morning. The cloud would have lifted to where it belonged around the tops of the peaks, and we would be able to see the wide opening of the Tari Gap again.

The Tari trip was always a bit of a lottery one way or another. I recall one occasion when there were just two of us onboard: the pilot, Dick, and myself. We had a full load of gear that we were ferrying back to Mendi. We were in the twin-engine Piper Aztec and grinding our way up out of Tari heading for the Gap. As usual I was in the right-hand seat. I often flew the planes myself from the co-pilot's seat when there was only the pilot and myself on board. This occurred more frequently if the pilot was getting over a hard night on the turps and needed to put his feet up and close his eyes for a while, especially on the early morning trip out of Mendi.

Anyway, this particular afternoon, we had gained altitude barely in time to sneak through the Gap just as the cloud came down behind us and closed it off. Just as we cleared the Gap, the port side engine sputtered and cut out. Dead! Dick tried to re-start it but to no avail.

Now we were in a bit of bother because we couldn't turn around and go back to Tari; the Gap had closed behind us. Neither could we gain any altitude, which was required when we needed to zig-zag around the mountain peaks to dodge the cloud and the hard bits. The Aztec only had small engines, and with a full load we could fly straight and level on one engine—but at the altitude we were flying, there was certainly not enough power to climb. There were also no airstrips closer than Mendi on which the Aztec could land.

Hurriedly, we got the flight map out and planned a longer, round-about route through the mountains further to the east and south, which would enable us to fly straight and level until we could lose altitude and land at Mendi. The cloud cover was constantly dropping at that time of day, and there were a lot of dead end valleys and guts en-route with a lot of hard bits sticking up! With seat-of-the pants flying, however, we eventually made it home in one piece.

Keeping Odd Company at Mt Hagen

Not long after my arrival in Mendi, I bought a long wheel-base Toyota Land Cruiser station wagon from a nun at a Catholic Mission Station between Mendi and Mt Hagen. It was a good wagon, and of course it was four-wheel drive, which was necessary in the Highlands. Every couple of weeks or so I would drive the two hours from Mendi to Mt Hagen to spend the weekend with friends and get a bit of social life of which there wasn't much in Mendi.

Dave Miles, the eldest son of friends from my Tairua Forest (New Zealand) days, lived in Mt Hagen. Dave was a pilot for Ansett PNG, based out of Mt Hagen. Also living in Mt Hagen was another Kiwi called Doug, who had been working on the Highlands Highway project for Dillinghams but who was now managing a rock quarry that Dave owned near Mt Hagen. Dave and Doug were good company, and we spent many pleasant Saturday afternoons drinking SP at Dave's place and socialising with other friends who called around.

Dave had a huge Hi-Fi system with massive speakers, which took up most of one room of his house. We would sit out on the verandah in his saggy old rattan chairs, with a chilly bin full of ice-cold SP, telling lies and listening to music. Our favourite song of the time was "American Pie" by Don McLean. It was a long song at eight minutes 42 seconds, and we played it over and over again.

The other reason that I visited Mt Hagen on a regular basis was to spend time with one of the most interesting ladies I have ever met. Her name was Tara Monahan. Tara was about 10 years older than me, and she had crammed so many incredible adventures into her 38 years that I never tired of listening to stories about her experiences. Tara was a complex and fiercely independent lady who had always lived on her own, by choice, and she was a white New Guinean through and through.

Tara had lived in PNG for most of her life. Her father had gone to PNG to work a plantation, taking his wife and young daughter with him. Christened Joyce Higginbotham, Tara later took her grandmother's maiden name of Monahan. It was the local Kukukuku people of Menyamya who gave her the name "Tara".

Tara went to school in Australia before returning to PNG to work in various government departments, municipalities, and private businesses. Tara gained quite a reputation in many careers over her lifetime and was one of PNG's great characters. She died in 1990 in Mt Hagen at age 54. Her obituary records her as having worked as an adjunct patrol officer, interpreter, pilot, naturalist, wildlife advocate, museum curator, artefact collector, tour organiser, and lastly as the manager of *Haus Poroman Lodge*.

Tara was the first woman to climb both Mt Wilhelm and Mt Otto in PNG and certainly the first woman (possibly the first person) to climb the Star Mountains, the most remote and inhospitable place on the entire PNG-West Papua Island. The Star Mountains run from the PNG-West Papua border well into Indonesian West Papua (previously known as Irian Jaya) as far as the remote Baliem Valley. Tara apparently climbed from the PNG end of the Star Mountain Range and across the mountains into Indonesian controlled territory— all quite illegally. She had two little white terriers that she loved dearly and credited with saving her life on more than one occasion during her time in the Star Mountains.

Tara had a red Morris Mini-Moke jeep that she drove everywhere, and Dave, Doug, and the Mt Hagen boys bet me early on that she would never let me drive it; she had never let anyone drive that thing. I drove Tara's Mini-Moke into Dave's driveway one Saturday afternoon for one of our weekend sessions about 3 months later, however. Tara had asked me to pick her up at about five o'clock from her travel agency office, so although I had won the bet she was still in control of the situation.

Tara was an attractive redhead and one tough lady with a very strong personality, and we had a lot in common and became close friends. She would have been hard work to live with though!

I narrowly avoided a spot of bother in Mt Hagen that was none of my making, but which was due to some of the company that I kept there. Doug had been doing the wild thing with Tina, the Mt Hagen Police Chief's lovely wife, while the Chief was away on patrol. Apparently the two had been at it for some time. The policeman had found out about it and had sent a message to Doug to cease and desist, but the warning had fallen on deaf ears.

A week before one of my visits to Mt Hagen, the less than devoted wife, Tina, had flown the family coop and was believed to be staying at Tara's place while continuing to have it away with Doug.

On this particular evening in Mt Hagen, I had just walked out of a local bar where I had been having a beer with an acquaintance when I was confronted by an extremely large and irate policeman. I had met Big Sam, the Police Chief, a few times, and I knew him well enough to chat to. Sam had discovered that I knew Doug and that I regularly spent time with him and Dave when I came over from Mendi. On this night, Big Sam had consumed more than a few SP lagers, and he was not a happy chappy.

He started in with, "Ross, you tell that scummy Kiwi mate of yours that if he so much as looks at Tina again I will be sending a squad of Tolai policemen to rearrange his features, and if they rearrange them permanently then I will not be unhappy. You go and tell him that!"

Discretion being the better part of valour, I answered, "Yeah Sam, I'll be sure to tell him. I'll make sure that he gets the message."

I hurried straight back to Dave's place, but Doug wasn't there. Dave reckoned that he had a good idea where Doug was—and what he was doing! I told Dave what Sam had told me, and I asked him to give Doug the message when he caught up with him. Next morning, I high-tailed it back to Mendi, and I didn't come back to Mt Hagen for about a month, hoping that by then everything would have blown over. I decided that I didn't need to get involved in that sort of argy bargy.

Payback!

Papua New Guineans do not accept natural causes as an explanation for misfortunes such as sickness, accidents, or death. Instead these are attributed to supernatural causes, which are grouped under the collective term of *sanguma* or sorcery. Those accused of sorcery are considered to have deliberately caused misfortune through the use of supernatural powers.

The prescribed punishment or payback to be meted out to anyone accused of killing or injuring a pig, a man, a *pikinini*, or a *meri* (in this order of importance to a Highland native), is usually death. Payback punishment can also include severe injury, however, such as hacking off a limb, shooting an arrow or two into various parts of the body, or burning down the perpetrator's house or entire village often with the people still inside.

Although these traditional punishments may seem harsh to the outsider, the severity, inventiveness, and savagery of payback punishment in the years following independence (1975), and right up to the present day, make those traditional retributions of the past seem like a Sunday School picnic. With independence came self-rule which was soon followed by total anarchy. There is practically no law now in PNG except the law of the *raskols* (urban criminal gangs), the *Sangumas*, and every bad bugger who can command a gang or a following to execute another payback.

Police and anecdotal reports from expatriates who have worked in PNG recently, confirm that paybacks now include beheadings with a *busnaip* (machete), strangling to death, being buried alive, having the skin flayed off the face and then being tied up to die slowly and painfully, thrown over a cliff, forced to drink petrol, and shot or stoned to death.

Inter-tribal fighting has been the traditional method of exacting payback for perceived sorcery, wife stealing, rape, or any other wrongs believed to have been committed by a member of one tribe against another, since time immemorial. Most payback disputes, before independence in 1975, were traditionally settled with strictly observed rules, using bows and arrows, clubs and spears. Unfortunately, after independence came modernisation and anarchy, with the use of guns, grenades, and guerrilla tactics. The total lawlessness and savagery of the *raskols* has overridden any traditional chivalry that may have existed previously.

In 1973, however, the payback system was still relatively "civilised" and traditional in the Southern Highlands. It worked like this: Hundreds of years ago, Tribe A, which lived on one side of a ridge, captured, killed, and ate a *meri* belonging to Tribe B, which lived on the other side of the ridge. Some-time later (it might be weeks, months, or years), when the *Sanguma* considered that the spirits were in alignment, Tribe B would carry out a raid on a Tribe A's village, fire a few arrows and spears, and kill or wound someone from Tribe A. This was a satisfactory outcome for both sides, as Tribe B got their payback and had now achieved justice, and Tribe A (having lived in constant expectation of the payback from Tribe B) had repaid the blood debt.

Now, however, it was the turn of tribe A to obtain payback from Tribe B for the raid on the village, and so on, and so on, until today and on into the future. Each tribe knew which tribes they owed payback to, but the original reason was often lost in the mists of time and was no longer relevant anyway. It had simply became a way of life.

Early one Saturday morning, I was driving my Land Cruiser from Mendi to Mt Hagen along the narrow, dusty apology for a highway. The road was really only a single lane with a few wider passing areas, and on the stretch that I was travelling it ran along the crest of a narrow ridge. It was a misty morning in the mountains; the mist was rising from the lower lying land on each side of the road, and visibility was limited. The land on either side of the road was owned by two different tribes, and there had been reports from the Mendi Patrol Officers that there had been signs of unrest in the area for some time. Nothing untoward had occurred to date, however, so I wasn't concerned and was driving along with the windows open, peering ahead, and keeping a close eye on the road through the mist. The next minute…WHANG! Something hit the Land Cruiser.

"What the hell was that?" I thought.

I couldn't see anything much through the mist, but suddenly something else hit the wagon and my windscreen wiper disappeared in front of my eyes. Then there was lot of shouting and whoo-whooing from both sides of the ridge before I received a couple more hits on my wagon.

As the mist thinned out a bit I saw a horde of painted, feathered tribesmen with bows and arrows lined up along each side of the ridge below the road, and they were lobbing arrows blindly at each other. I was desperately trying to wind my windows up, stay on the road, and speed up, all at the same time!

Then both sides spotted me simultaneously. Someone shouted to cease fire as there was a *Masta* driving along the road. Hostilities ceased, and someone shouted at me to drive on through.

I needed no further encouragement and obliged wholeheartedly. As soon as I was out of missile range, I slowed down to look behind me and saw that arrows were once again being lobbed over the road as if nothing had happened. When I got back to Mendi on the Monday morning, I found out that there had been a payback battle scheduled for the Saturday morning because one tribe needed to score a hit on the guys on the other side of the ridge to even up the payback score.

Apparently, someone got an arrow through the shoulder not long after I had driven through. The tribe that had fired the arrow declared victory, and everyone stopped firing and went back home again. That's just the way it goes in the Highlands!

I ended up with a couple of small dents in the door of the wagon from arrow hits, and I had to buy myself a new windscreen wiper arm in Mt Hagen, but I counted myself lucky that an arrow hadn't found its way through the open window before I had managed to wind it up or I could have lost more than a wiper arm. Needless to say, I felt it wise not to seek payback for the damage to my Land Cruiser!

"Liberating" the Margarima *Yupin*

Late in 1972, I received a letter from the National Museum in Wellington, New Zealand, about the collection of New Guinea artefacts that I had previously loaned to the museum. The curators explained that the collection was particularly valuable to them, as it comprised a good proportion of the total collection of Papua New Guinean artefacts held by the museum at that time. They would be extremely grateful, they wrote, if I would agree to donate the collection to the museum permanently.

Because I was living and working away from New Zealand for an indefinite period, I felt it was a sensible move for me to donate my collection permanently to the National Museum where it would be appreciated and studied and would contribute to the museum's knowledge of the ethnology and cultures of PNG. So I agreed to their request.

When he learned that I was then living in the Southern Highlands, Roger Neich (still Curator of Pacific Ethnology), started corresponding with me. He hoped that I might find myself in a position to track down and obtain some significant and rare artefacts that he and the museum were particularly keen to get their hands on. His wish-list included prehistoric mortars and pestles that pre-dated the present tribal cultures of PNG, and (most especially) a *yupin* basketwork fertility figure from the Southern Highlands—if I could find one. Even some photos and some background information would be extremely valuable to the museum,

Roger wrote, as he felt it very unlikely that I could obtain an actual *yupin* figure.

Roger was doing a detailed study of the *yupin* figures. He wrote that they were extremely rare, but as I tended to travel into the more remote regions of the Highlands, Roger knew that I would have more chance of finding a *yupin* than most collectors given my profession and my personal interest in ethnology. He told me that the museum would be more than happy to pay me for anything that I could supply.

I had always been on the lookout for interesting items during my travels, but now that I had a list and guidelines on what the museum was specifically looking for, I started collecting in earnest. I collected some very old *kundu* drums, human hair wigs of the Huli wigmen, and a number of ancient mortars and pestles from the more remote villages around the Southern Highlands. The latter originated from a culture or civilisation that pre-dated and was unknown to the present people of the Southern Highlands.

It was now well into 1973, and I had still not located a *yupin* figure, although I had asked and enquired everywhere I went. No-one was prepared to even talk about them, leave alone indicate where I might find one. This was apparently because *yupin* figures were believed to be full of magic, and when a *yupin* had accumulated so much spiritual power, it was deemed to be too powerful and dangerous for the tribe. It was then taken out into the jungle by the *Sanguma* or *Luri Luri Man* (witch-doctor) and abandoned in the forest. It then returned to the spirit world from whence it came. The native people were afraid of these figures, and even to talk about them was against their custom.

Not long before I left Mendi, I was having a yarn with Duna, my foreman who was in charge of the forest nursery at Margarima. Margarima is a village high up in the mountains of the Southern Highlands at 2,560 metres above sea level, and it was very cold up there at night. The cloud and misty rain often came down over the Margarima valley from about 3 p.m., and things could get pretty miserable. I had been stuck there overnight a few times when the plane couldn't get back into Margarima to pick me up because of the weather, and I had learned to always carry a pair of long trousers and a warm jersey whenever I flew there.

This particular night I had been stranded yet again, and I would be staying the night in a native hut on the edge of the village not far from the nursery. Now I was sitting by a fire eating fire blackened *kaukau* with Duna and his family.

We got around to discussing *yupin* figures and the stories surrounding them. Duna became a bit more informative about the *yupins* once his wife and family had departed from around the fire.

I was most interested to discover that there was a very old *yupin* figure in the old Margarima Government Council House nearby. The old Council House, which also doubled as the *Haus Tambaran* (spirit house), was highly sacred and was totally off limits to women and children. In fact, ordinarily no-one could enter a *Haus Tambaran* other than the *Sanguma,* the councillors, and the elders. I couldn't believe that I was so close to a *yupin* but couldn't get to see it, so I asked Duna to introduce me to the caretaker of the Council House.

It turned out that the big man who had all the say around the Council House and *Haus Tambaran* was the local

Sanguma, and so we went into the village to find him. Sitting around his fire and chewing *buai* (betel nut), the *Sanguma* and I soon became good mates. He agreed to explain to me some of the history of the Margarima *yupin* and how the figure was used in the Huli traditions.

Late in the night he told me a very interesting thing that made my ears really prick up. The Margarima *yupin* was very, very old, and had been used for so many years and had accumulated so much magic and power that the tribe had become afraid to use it. The *Sanguma* was soon about to take it out into the bush and release it to the jungle, as was the custom. He agreed to take me to the old Council House the next day to let me see the *yupin* for myself. I got very little sleep that night what with the portent of what I might see the next day coupled with the very cold temperatures in the mountains.

The next day, my new friend the *Sanguma* led me to the old Council House, which was not far from the end of the airstrip and somewhat apart from the main village. The Council House was an old, traditional round house made of woven bamboo and mud, with a raised *kunai* grass roof. The inside of the thatched ceiling was black and tarry from the smoky fires that had burned in the centre of the floor for many years, and there was dust and grime everywhere.

The *Sanguma* brought a bamboo ladder from the back of the building, and he propped it up among the rafters. There were numerous racks containing *kundu* drums, bamboo matting, and other stuff up among the rafters, and soon he was crawling around amongst all this. Eventually, he came back down the ladder carrying the mysterious *yupin* under one arm.

The shivers ran up my spine to finally see this little chap that I had heard so much about and that so many people would apparently give their eye teeth to get their hands on. The figure was about 70 centimetres high, and the head and chest were about 80 centimetres in circumference. He appeared to be made of tightly woven rattan cane, which had darkened from the smoke in the ceilings where he had been stored. He had a face mask made of some sort of gourd, which was stained yellow and red. He may have lost other decorative features over time, due to his age, but he still had a small black resin nose, and a black beard and hair fashioned from tightly curled human hair that had been stuck around the edge of the mask.

The *Sanguma* explained in quite some detail the origins and uses of this particular *yupin*, and that this *yupin* was unique in its purposes within his tribal group. He told me that this *yupin* had originally come from Yaruna Village. This *yupin* was apparently ancient, and was likely to have been made before missionaries had set foot in the region. It was unknown how long the *yupin* figure had been stored in Margarima's old Council House.

The figure was usually called a *taama*, but its name changed to *amena* whenever it was used in a pig-killing ceremony. The figure would have been woven by several men from bush vines and cane strips gathered from the forest. Although the *taama* would normally be kept in an especially built *Haus Tambaran* built from bush materials, this one was stored in the old Council House because that building also served as the *Haus Tambaran* for the village.

The *Sanguma* made it clear that only men were permitted to carry, touch, or even look upon the *yupin* figure, whether it was in the *Haus Tambaran* or being carried outside, or in the Council House. When it was used in a pig-killing ceremony, the men would carry the *amena* around the village for the entire night. No-one would sleep. At sunrise, the figure would be returned to his house. The pigs would then be killed, and the *sing sing* (traditional dancing and singing) would begin. He also told me a little about the initiation of teenage boys in the tribe, and how the figure, as *taami* was used.

Having heard the *Sanguma's* stories, I knew that I had to try to obtain this little guy and somehow get him back to Wellington for Roger and his ethnologists to examine. So, I started negotiating with the *Sanguma*. I suggested to him that if he was going to take the *yupin* out into the jungle to rot and remove him from the tribal environment, why not let me save him the trouble? I could remove him to a place far away, and he could make a few dollars in the process. If we wrapped him in something, I could get him onto the plane when it arrived, and no-one in the village would be any the wiser. He thought about this, and we argued back and forth at some length, but in the end my powers of persuasion and three A$20 notes did the trick, and we shook hands on a deal.

As we had to do the deed without any of the villagers becoming aware, I wrapped the *yupin* in my sleeping *laplap* and a spare shirt that I had in my bag, and we waited until we heard the plane circling above the airfield in preparation for landing. The *Sanguma* went outside to check if anyone was around and, when he was satisfied that we weren't being watched, he signalled to me. I quickly exited the old Council House and trotted off across the airfield to the plane with my prize under my arm

The pilot had seen me coming and had left the engine running, so I opened the back door, threw my bag and my precious cargo in the back, jumped into the co-pilot's seat, and told him to get moving. Once airborne, I had to make up a story to satisfy the pilot as to the nature of the strange looking, smoky-smelling bundle that I had stowed behind his seat. I didn't want the whole world knowing that I had kidnapped a *yupin*!

A few weeks later I prepared to leave Mendi and PNG with my *yupin* in an old suitcase that I had scrounged off someone. I packed the rest of my artefacts (including the mortars and pestles) into boxes and headed back to New Zealand before taking up a new job in Borneo, Indonesia.

When I arrived in Auckland, I hired a car and drove to Wellington with my treasures. Roger and the team were over the moon when they saw what I had brought back. I stayed in Wellington for a few days so I could de-brief them on the origins and stories associated with each item—especially the *yupin*. They offered to pay me for what I had collected, but I only accepted enough to cover the actual cost of purchase. Then I headed to New Plymouth to visit the folks, then to Auckland, and finally on to Indonesia.

Some months later, I received a copy of Roger's paper on the *yupin* figures entitled "Basketwork Fertility Figures from The Western Enga and Nearby Groups, Western and Southern Highlands, Papua New Guinea". In it, Roger noted that the *yupin* I had liberated from the Margarima Council house was "the only one known to have belonged to a Huli-speaking group. In nearly all respects it is a typical Enga *yupin* figure." Apparently, the information that I had passed along from the *Sanguma* was the only evidence ethnologists had that *yupin* figures were associated with boys' initiation rituals.

In 1975, PNG gained its independence, or rather had independence forced upon it by the talking heads at the United Nations (UN). PNG then formed what is questionably referred to as a government and started to flex its "independence muscle". One of the things that it did early on was to send out envoys from the Papua New Guinea Museum to nearby countries that wanted to become "friends" for political and strategic purposes. These "friends", particularly Australia and New Zealand, were seen as soft touches. The PNG envoys were searching the overseas museums for any PNG artefacts that they felt were rare and desirable enough to repatriate back to their own national museum in Port Moresby.

An item printed in the *Pacific Islands Monthly* magazine dated June 1975, immediately following PNG's independence, trumpeted the headlines on page 35 in the PNG news section: "Homecoming for Yupin".

> A collection of rare cultural pieces taken out of Papua New Guinea two years ago has been handed over to the Papua New Guinea Public Museum and Art Gallery by the New Zealand National Museum. The collection includes pre-historic stone mortars and pestles and a rare wickerwork figure, yupin, which was once used in initiation ceremonies in the Western Enga area between the Southern and Western Highlands. It is the first time that an overseas museum has returned cultural property to Papua New Guinea. Curator of Ethnology at the New Zealand National Museum, Mr Roger Neich, presented the collection in April to the Director of the Papua New Guinea

Public Museum and Art Gallery, Mr Geoffrey Mosuwadoga.

The yupin figure in particular has great cultural importance for Papua New Guinea. Mr Neich who has made a comprehensive study of yupin figures, believes it documents the spread of Western Enga yupin figures into the Huli language area and that it is one of only a dozen in the world, five of which are now held by the Papua New Guinea Museum. The National Museum, New Zealand, bought the collection a year ago. Most of the pieces are from the Southern Highlands. The yupin is from Yaruna village and has a gourd face mask typical of Southern Highlands craft. It was used in rituals by groups from Western Enga, Ipili and Pai-Ela.

In hindsight, if I had known that these artefacts may have been returned to PNG in this manner, I would have had second thoughts about giving or selling them to the New Zealand National Museum. I would have certainly loaned them to Roger and the ethnology team, but I should have retained ownership which may have made it more difficult for the items to be repatriated.

The house I had built for myself at the Ewasse Government Station, 1972.

Bialla airstrip, West New Britain, 1972.

Ulumona log yard, West New Britain coast, 1972. Father *Buai's* sawmill is on the left, and Mt Ulawun (2,280 metres) towers in the background.

Huli wigmen at a *'sing sing'*, Tari Basin, 1973.

A Huli widow in mourning. Tari area, 1973.

An airstrip in the Southern Highlands, 1973. The young pilots who flew into such precarious airstrips were nicknamed "the kamikaze boys".

Missionary Aviation Fellowship (MAF) plane on a village airstrip. Southern Highland 1973.

The Tari Gap, approaching from the Mendi side on a fine morning. Its apparent tranquility on a day like this belies its danger. Southern Highlands, 1973.

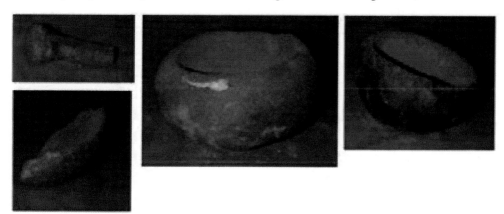

Some of the pre-historic mortars and pestles collected by the author and donated to the National Museum of New Zealand in 1973.

Photo courtesy of Sean Mallon, Te Papa Museum, Wellington, NZ.

A Highlands village between Mendi and Mt Hagen, Southern Highlands, 1972.

Sanguma (witchdoctor). Tari District, Southern Highlands, 1973. Witchdoctors are both feared and respected in their villages.

The Margarima *yupin* that the author collected in 1973.
Photo by David Becker and supplied courtesy of Barry Craig, South Australia Museum

Time to Leave PNG

In early 1973, it became clear that PNG was being forced along the path to independence. I knew from day one that being thrust into independence and self-government at this stage of the country's development could mean nothing but disaster for PNG, a country that I had grown to love. It was a wonderful country, a man's country, an honest country with fascinating people and a place that I would willingly have lived and worked in for many more years. But you can't drag people out of the Stone Age, hand them western democracy and self-government one week then abandon them to their fate the next. It should never have happened like that. In 1973, the fallout from independence was all in the future, but I could see the signs, and I knew it was time for me to move on.

Police instructions had been issued that any expatriate driving in the Highlands who had an accident and hit a native man, *meri*, *pikinini*, or pig, whether causing a serious injury or even just a bump, must not stop under any circumstances. To stop at an accident was now against the law. The driver must drive with all speed straight to the nearest police station, no matter how far away it was, and report the incident to the police. If any natives near the incident saw or recognised the vehicle or recorded the plate number, then the expatriate would need to be on a flight out of the country within the week, or the natives would track him down and kill him. If the driver stopped at the scene of the accident, even to attempt to save a life, he would be killed on the spot. No ifs; no buts. The payback system had already started to evolve with the coming of independence.

I put the word out on the international Forestry grapevine that I was looking at leaving PNG sometime before the final date of independence in 1975. I wasn't fussy about the timing, and I was quite happy to continue to live and work in the country until such time as something suitable (and better) came up elsewhere. I would have liked to have spent at least another year in Mendi if possible, but I was easy.

Within a month of putting the word out, however, I had received two offers of good positions. The first offer was Forestry Manager for Direct Transport in Rotorua, New Zealand, which involved managing and scheduling a fleet of logging trucks in the central North Island. A few days later, I was offered the position of Forestry Manager for the Usutu Pulp Company in Swaziland. The Swaziland job sounded more interesting, and the salary was considerably higher, and with full expatriate conditions.

As I have said, I was in no hurry to leave Mendi, but the offers were time-limited, so I thought about it and accepted the Swaziland job. I had only just mailed my acceptance letter when I got a phone call from my old mate Jim Riley from Bulolo days, who was, at that time, working as a consultant for J.G. Groome and Associates, Forestry Consultants in Rotorua, New Zealand. The company's principal, John Groome, had been contacted by the big American forestry corporation, Weyerhaeuser, concerning a vacancy with its subsidiary in Indonesia. John had heard on the grapevine that I was in the market for a move and asked

Jim if he would track me down to see if I would be interested in the job in East Kalimantan.

When Jim called me, I asked him, "Where the hell is East Kalimantan?"

I had never heard of it. He told me that it was in Indonesian Borneo. I knew nothing about Indonesia—in fact I only vaguely knew where it was! He said the position was Raw Materials Supervisor for International Timber Corporation Indonesia (ITCI), which was managed and majority owned by Weyerhaeuser.

Having just accepted the Swaziland job and knowing nothing about Indonesia, I said I needed to think about it, and I asked him to call me back in a few days.

I asked around Mendi to see if anyone knew anything about Indonesia, but the only information I could gather was from some of the Aussie bush pilots.

They told me, "Hey mate, you don't want to go there. That place is totally lawless and full of head-hunters and cannibals!"

Here I was, comfortably living in the Southern Highlands of Papua, chewing betel nut with cannibals and witchdoctors, only to be told that this Indonesia place was wilder even than "home". What to do?

When Jim phoned me up again, I told him, "Sorry mate, I've already accepted this job in Swaziland and, from what I hear, I don't like the sound of Indonesia, so I've decided to turn the opportunity down."

Two days later, John Groome himself phoned me to tell me that ITCI had offered to fly me from Mendi to Port Moresby to East Kalimantan, via Singapore, to have a look at the job, the location, the people, and the management. They would then fly me back home to Mendi via Manila in the Philippines—say two weeks all up, all expenses paid, and no obligation. I could make my decision when I got back to Mendi.

Well, it was a bit difficult to turn down a two-week holiday, covering three countries that I had never been to, with all expenses paid and no strings attached, so I said, "OK, you're on. When do I leave?"

The rest, as they say, is history. I fell in love with Indonesia on my first day in Samarinda on the Mahakam River in East Kalimantan. I loved the food, the people, the river, the jungle, the job—and the Company was good. But the icing on the cake had to be all the beautiful Indonesian girls. They were everywhere! I figured that I must have died and gone to heaven.

It turned out that the only Indonesia that the bush pilots in Mendi knew about was the Eastern and most lawless side of Irian Jaya (West Papua). They had been flying around and across the PNG-Irian Jaya border between Vanimo and Jayapura and other outback airstrips where the country was wild and the law was vague to say the least. The difference between the Indonesia that they knew and the "real" Indonesia on the western side of the "Wallace Line" was like comparing Earth with Mars.

After a week in Kalimantan, I flew back to Singapore, then to Manila where I stayed five days in the Marco Polo Hotel, all at ITCI's expense. I went to the Jai Lai (Pelota) and lost money, I went to the cock fights and won money, and I checked out some of the lovely Filipina girls while I was there. I arrived back in Mendi, and for some reason my little haven up there in the Southern Highlands of PNG just didn't seem so inviting anymore.

John phoned me again when I got home and offered me a very good salary package with free accommodation, no tax, ten days leave in Singapore every two months (all expenses paid), free flights back to New Zealand every year, and all sorts of other good stuff. So I "reluctantly" told him, "I'm on my way to Indonesia, John, much obliged!"

I resigned from the PNG Department of Forests, resigned from the position that I had previously accepted in Swaziland, and spent a month training up a new local Papuan DFO in Mendi. I flew back to New Zealand for two weeks to drop off the recently acquired additions to my artefact collection at the National Museum in Wellington and visit the folks in New Plymouth. Then I was off to Singapore and a whole new life in Indonesia!

I had lived in Papua New Guinea for over five years from 1967 to 1973, which included the final years of Australian administration. PNG was then a wonderful country—primarily a primitive, almost Stone Age, culture, but well administered, safe, nominally law abiding (apart from millennia old tribal warfare), and totally uncorrupted. The people were fascinating, and in most cases, worldly innocent. I had wandered at will through jungles and villages all over the country, stayed the night in many, followed my profession as a forester and my interest in primitive ethnology, and rarely did I hear of, or experience, any threat against expatriates. It was a great country to live and work in, and under the Australian administration the populace had the freedom to continue with their age old culture and customs, meanwhile improving and developing at a rate at which they could handle.

Independence and western style government was, in effect, forced on Papua New Guinea by the United Nations. So-called free elections were held in 1972 and 1973 (while I was living in the Southern Highlands), with the pre-ordained result that PNG would become independent and self-governing from the 16th of September 1975. In the villages which could be readily contacted (which were a minority), the illiterate, uneducated village chiefs, were instructed to put their thumb prints on the pro-independence voting paper by the UN pollsters on behalf of their entire village. These people had as much idea of what independence and self-government entailed as if they had been asked if they wanted to emigrate to the moon. I know, because I was there at the time and witnessed some farcical episodes in some of the villages.

One chief in a village which I was visiting when the UN people arrived, proclaimed, when asked if he wanted independence, *"Mipela i laik forpela independans — wanpela independans bilong mipela, wanpela bilong meri bilong mi, wanpela bilong pikinini man bilong mi, na wanpela bilong pikinini meri bilong mi"*. Translated, he said that he wanted four independences: "One for me, one for my wife, one for my son, and one for my daughter." He was being offered something for nothing, and as no one looks a gift horse in the mouth, he reckoned he would have as many of them as were on offer – whatever they were. He didn't understand the first thing about independence or its repercussions, and neither would he be expected to. That episode, which I know from other first-hand reports, was repeated with variations, throughout the country, and in effect, encapsulated the so-called UN referendum for PNG independence. The result was a farcical but overwhelming and pre-determined vote for almost immediate independence and self-government. There was little, if any, thought or consideration given to the critical fact that a primitive culture would need assistance, guidance, and special arrangements over an extended period in order to process the change from a benign and effective administration to a system of government and self-rule that would be quite different, and in effect, foreign, to the entire population.

The reality today, unfortunately, is a country that is plagued by anarchy, tribal warfare (now using AK47s instead of bows and arrows), criminal gangs (known as *raskols*) terrorising the population, breakdown of law and order, and government corruption. The government consists of representatives from about 60 tribal and language groups, but the other 640 odd tribal groups don't recognise their "authority". Dodgy foreign business interests have paid off politicians so that they can carry out their dubious activities, and blatantly rape and pillage the country of its natural resources. The local landowners and villagers in the areas where these activities take place, get little or no benefit from the development around them.

In the cities, the employees of genuine companies that have invested in the country and are trying to carry out legitimate business, are forced to live behind electrified fences with guard dogs and armed security.

Meanwhile, up in the Highlands and out in the jungle, life carries on largely as it has for thousands of years.

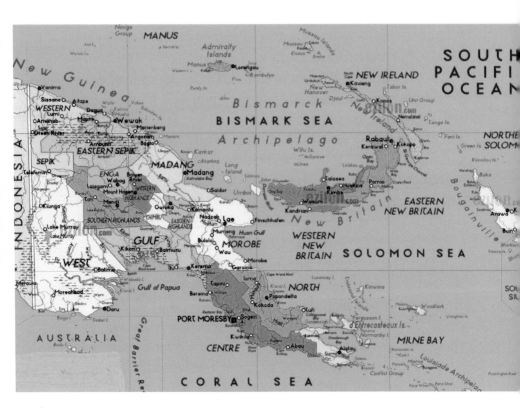

Map of Papua New Guinea